Introduction to Innovation

Volume 3

Stability and Innovation

Jon-Arild Johannessen

Copyright © 2016 Author Name

All rights reserved.

ISBN-13:
978-1537076645

ISBN-10:
1537076647

DEDICATION

To my wife

CONTENTS

Introduction to innovation-The volumes in the serie 6
Volume 1: Theory 6
Volume 2: Innovation and Entrepreneurship 6
Volume 3: Stability and Innovation 6
Volume 4: Historical introduction to innovation 6
CHAPTER 1 STABILITY AND CHANGE 7
REFERENCES 34
CHAPTER 2 CRITICAL INNOVATION FACTORS 38
REFERENCES 64
CHAPTER 3 INNOVATION AND PERCOLATION 79
REFERENCES 115
Chapter on concepts 137
INDEX 174
ABOUT THE AUTHOR 177

Stability and Innovation

Introduction to innovation-The volumes in the serie

Volume 1: Theory

Volume 2: Innovation and Entrepreneurship

Volume 3: Stability and Innovation

Volume 4: Historical introduction to innovation

CHAPTER 1 STABILITY AND CHANGE

INTRODUCTION

The purpose of the chapter is to say something about the relation between organisational channel capacity and innovation. The purpose is further to investigate how the flow of information and a communicative environment in an organisation can lead to increased stability (of the variability at the individual level) and at the same time high innovation behaviour.

Several authors contend that an open communicative environment and free flow of information promote innovation processes in organisations. Among these authors are Rogers & Shoemaker (1972), Kanter (1983), Rotwell (1991), Rogers (1983), Kahn & Manopichetwattana (1989), Jarillo (1988) and MacMillan (1983).

The actors in such contexts find it easier to get in touch with others, both for support and criticism of personal points of view. They will also in a more direct way be able to make use of other people's special knowledge. In this border area between different kinds of expertise, the innovative ideas will much more easily develop. Such an environment will further facilitate the link between theory and practice, too. In such an encounter practical experience and theoretical knowledge will more easily serve the organisation as a whole.

A condition for this to happen, is that the organisation develops a communication policy ,furthering complementary relationships, i.e. relationships where basic trust exists, and where a helping and supportive basic attitude is the cornerstone (Johannessen & Hauan, 1993).

The open communicative environment is further based on the condition that communication can take place both vertically, horizontally, and diagonally in the organisation. A bureaucratic style of administration must on these grounds be avoided, if innovation is the focus of attention.

Several investigations show that the degree of innovation in organisations emphasising written communication is less than in organisations promoting face-to-face communication (Kanter, 1983; Burns & Stalker, 1968). The explanation to this could be the speed at which ideas are spread, immediate feedback, and correction will take place more easily with face-to-face communication, than with the use of formal written procedures. Kanter (1983:189) makes the following explicit statement: "Open communication serves a very important function for the potential innovator". The open communicative environment metaphorically opens the eyes to our own blindness, which in itself can be regarded as an act of innovation.

An open communicative environment built on complementary relationships paves the way for information not being used as a fight for strategic positions in order to serve own interests at the expense of the interests of the total system. Examples in literature of information games where the actors use information to serve their own interests at the expense of the total interest of the organisation, are to be found with Krehbiel (1987), Sheprle & Weingast (1987) and March & Olsen (1989).

The chapter is organised in the following manner: First we shall determine the technical term channel capacity in organisational terms. Then we shall look at the relation between organisational channel capacity and innovation: Then comes an examination of the relation between channel capacity and stability in an organisation. We shall also make use of a thought experiment to apply Ashby's "connectance" concept to organisational change processes, and link the concept to organisational channel capacity to explain the relation between change at the partial system level and stability at the total system level. In our conclusion we shall outline certain management implications on the basis of the argumentation in the chapter.

ORGANISATIONAL CHANNEL CAPACITY

To determine the concept organisational channel capacity, we use the concepts information flow and communication environment. Fig. 1 is developed to visualise the concept of organisational channel capacity.

Fig. 1 organisational channel capacity

	Information flow	
	Free	Limited
Open (Communication environment)	Large organizational channel capacity — 1	Average organizational channel capacity — 2
Closed	Average organizational channel capacity — 3	Small organizational channel capacity — 4

Free flow of information here means that information flows freely in the organisation. This applies both to internal and external information. The only limitation the free flow of information is subject to in the model, is information particularly sensitive to the organisation, and thus potentially harmful to the organisation if made accessible to persons not concerned.

Limited flow of information here means that the information is subject to limitations of some kind, extending beyond the sensitive information. The limitations may be the very frequency of information, secretion of certain types of information being sent to certain groups, while other groups in the organisation are not given access to this type of information etc.

An open communicative environment means that everyone in principle has the opportunity to communicate with everyone. A closed communicative environment means that there are clear limitations on who can communicate with whom. This can for example be determined by regulations or be geographically determined.

Large organisational channel capacity is in the model determined by an open communicative environment, and free flow of information. Limited flow of information and an open communicative environment are in the model determining factors for average channel capacity. What narrows channel capacity, is limitations imposed on the flow of information. The channel has, on the other hand, a potential for extension, but this potential is not exploited due to limitations on the flow of information.

Free flow of information and a closed communicative environment also determine what we choose to denote as average channel capacity. Also this channel has the potential for larger organisational channel capacity which is not exploited due to various limitations on communication.

Small organisational channel capacity is here determined by the limited flow of information and a closed communicative environment. Here there are both limitations on the very information flowing through the organisation, and the communication between the actors. This channel does not have the potential for larger organisational channel capacity.

Small organisational channel capacity will lean towards an hierarchical organisational structure and a partly authoritarian management. This is because authority from superior levels in the organisation will more easily develop without the possibility of corrections from lower levels.

Large channel capacity will tend towards an Heterarchical structure (Johannessen, 1991; Johannessen & Hauan, 1992; Hauan & Johannessen, !993), and the management will be democratic. This is because the open communicative environment will lead to self-regulations in the various parts of the organisation, and the open flow of information will hinder any possible exercise of authority from one or few persons.

Cell 2 in fig. 1 is characterised by a bureaucratic structure and a democratic management. The democratic element is seen in the fact that everyone in the organisation can communicate with each other, and thus modify authoritarian tendencies. The bureaucratic element is introduced in that certain limitations are imposed on the flow of information. This implies that certain explicit rules apply as to how information is to be administered in the organisation, which is a characteristic feature of bureaucratic organisation.

Cell 3 is characterised as distributed structure and "open" style of management. The distributed element comes in as a result of information flowing freely in the organisation, while there are obvious limitations on the opportunities for the actors to communicate with each other. If there is free flow of information, this should mean free communication between the actors. It is only in terms of definition to increase the frequency of the information flow, and an approximately open communicative environment will in principle exist. What is the case with cell 3, is that the organisation is divided geographically in that e.g. various divisions are located in different geographical areas. Among the various actors in these divisions, there can be no extensive face-to face communication, even if this can occur internally in the various divisions. In the various divisions where this might happen, these will be placed in cell 1 in the matrix. But if the entire organisation, e.g. the various divisions, is viewed as a whole, the channel capacity of the organisation will be average. We can not say anything in particular about the style of management in such an organisation, as management has little to do with geography. We will therefore put "open "style of management in this cell.

In the model a distinction is made between bureaucratic and hierarchical organisational structure. This we have done to show the distinction between the open and the closed communicative environment. The model says something about power structure, flow of information, and communicative environment.

What we are to look at now is: Can we by means of the concept organisational channel capacity say something about stability and invitational behaviour in organisations? If we are to find a positive connection between large organisational channel capacity and, at the same time, great organisational stability and a high degree of innovation behaviour, we have made a contribution to "the hopeless choice" in organisations, i.e. the supposed choice between stability and innovation.

THE RELATIONSHIP BETWEEN CHANNEL CAPACITY AND DEGREE OF INNOVATION.

If the organisational channel capacity in the organisation is large, the potential for idea generation will be great. This is because information will be coupled between the various actors of the organisation. The various actors with their previous knowledge get access both to information and communication with others in the organisation. In this meeting a potential for idea generation will develop. This meeting can also shorten the period of time from the moment an idea appears till a service is launched.

For average and small organisational channel capacity the argumentation is the same, as far as the potential for idea generation is concerned, with the exception that the potential for idea generation is respectively average or low.

In the concept organisational channel capacity we have not looked at the frequency of communication between the actors or the frequency of information flow in the organisation. The omission of one frequency in the concept of organisational channel capacity, is made to reduce the complexity of the concept.

If we look at the relationship between channel capacity and the frequency of communication and information, we will develop the following chain of arguments: If the organisational channel capacity is large and the frequency of the information flow is also large, the actors will have quicker access to information. The communication which is now intensive due to a high degree of communication between the actors, will further facilitate idea generation and the spreading of ideas in the organisation.

If both the organisational channel capacity and the frequency of interaction between the actors are too big, but the frequency of the information flow is average or low, the latter will impede the generation of ideas and the spreading of ideas. Further limitations will occur if the frequency of the information flow is too high, but the frequency of communication is too low. This is because generation of ideas and spreading of ideas is supposed to be constituted in the communicative meeting between the actors of the organisation. If both the frequency of communication and the flow of information are low, the spreading and generation of ideas will be strongly reduced. This is because the points of contact between the actors are minimal, and the information which should serve as the starting point for what is creatively new, is limited.

The relationship between organisational channel capacity and the two frequency targets, with regards to average and low organisational channel capacity, originate from the same series of argumentation. But the potential for the generation and spreading of ideas is declining for the organisation as a whole with falling channel capacity and falling frequency.

If the frequency of communication and information is high, it still need not say anything about the physical closeness between the actors. The frequency can be high even if the actors are geographically remote from each other. This possibility only increases with further use of various types of information and communication- related technology. If the physical distance between the actors in an organisation is small and the organisational channel capacity is large, the potential for generation of ideas is large, since this will promote face-to face communication. The more the physical distance increases, the smaller the possibility for face-to-face communication will be, and the potential for generation and spreading of ideas will decrease. Diminishing organisational channel capacity will have a negative effect on the potential for generation and spreading of ideas, parallel with increasing physical distance.

Even if the organisational channel capacity is large ,the frequency of communication between the actors is high, and the physical distance small, an important limitation on the potential for generation and spreading of ideas will be the type of relation which is developed in the organisation or part of it. If a symmetrical type of relation is dominant, competition, distrust, and protection of own ideas will be the dominating principle of action (Johannessen & Hauan, 1993; Johannessen & Olaisen, 1993). This type of relationship will then represent a type of limitation overshadowing the other positive entities previously discussed in relation to innovation.

Large organisational channel capacity, high frequency of information and communication, and little physical distance can be described as necessary pre-conditions for an innovative environment. But for the sufficient condition to come into play, complementary relationships must be developed in the entire organisation or part of it. By complementary relationships is here meant a basic trust between the actors, in addition to a helping and supportive basic attitude. A discussion of symmetrical and complementary relations is done by Johannessen & Hauan (1993), and put into a philosophy of science framework by Johannessen & Olaisen (1993).

As a general expression of the discussion so far, we have developed the following hypothesis: If the organisational channel capacity is large, and information and communication frequency is high, while the physical distance is small, and there are complementary relationships in parts of, or the entire organisation, the probability of a high innovation degree is large.

THE RELATIONSHIP BETWEEN ORGANISATIONAL CHANNEL CAPACITY AND STABILITY

Ashby (1970) asked the following question in an chapter in "Nature":

"If a large system is assembled (connected) at random, or has grown haphazardly, should we expect it to be stable or unstable? And how does the expectation change as n, the number of variables, tends to infinity?" Ashby points out in his chapter that the chances for the stability to decrease when the variables increase, are great, and possibly as fast as 2 squared in minus n. The results to which Ashby points, were from linear systems 100% connected, i.e. that changes in one variable has an immediate effect on the other variables.

Ashby in this chapter introduces the concept "connectance", which is the degree of connectedness percentage-wise, i.e. a change in one variable has an immediate effect on others, the connectance is 100%. If the change in one variable has no effect on the other variables, the connectance is 0%. Connectance thus varies between 0 and 100 percent. If the connectance is 10, it means that a change in one variable has an immediate effect of 10 percent on the other variables in the system. The conclusion Ashby arrived at in his studies, we have summarised in fig. 2.

Fig. 2 System stability

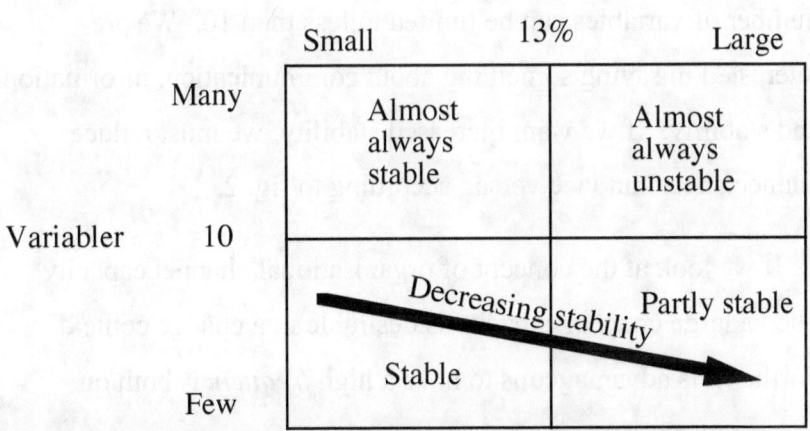

The model shows that a critical value for stability/instability in the system occurs when the connectance is 13%, and the number of variables (n) is 10. If we postulate that Ashby's connectance principle is a meta- design principle, we can ask the question: What implications does this principle have at the organisational level? We realise that a direct transfer of this principle to organisations is dubious, so the following line of thought is only meant as an analogy to Ashby's "connectance" concept. We think, however, that the analogy can explain something regarding the phenomenon we wish to say something about, namely organisational channel capacity and innovation.

In organisations the total number of variables will always be higher than 10. It is only in the modelling of organisations that the number of variables can be limited to less than 10. We are interested in saying something about communication, information, and stability. If we want increased stability, we must reduce connectance, and vice versa, according to fig. 2.

If we look at the concept of organisational channel capacity ,then a large channel capacity is desirable in a change context. Further it is advantageous to have a high *frequency* both on communication and information flow, in addition to small physical distance. If we suppose that the hypothesis we postulated at the end of part 3 is correct, then, if we use Ashby's "connectance" principle transferred to organisations with the uncertainty such an analogical interpretation entails, it will mean that "connectance" must be large to facilitate an increased degree of innovation". This implies, according to the "connectance" principle, that the system becomes unstable. It should be pointed out here that it is at individual and group level in organisations that the "connectance" principle is transferred, i.e. sub-system level in relation to the organisation as a whole. This means concretely that it is the sub-systems which are unstable when the organisational channel capacity is large and the frequency is high, and there is little physical distance between the actors.

The questions we shall ask are: Is it so that instability at sub-system level is necessarily the same as instability at organisational level? Is it conceivable that instability at sub-system level leads to stability at organisational level?

A Thought experiment

We imagine a group consisting of 13 persons. They have a structure of the information flow as shown in fig. 3. The communicative environment is defined as open, so that all thirteen in principle are able to communicate with everyone else. The frequency of information and communication is high, and there is substantial physical closeness among the persons. If these conditions are fulfilled, the analogical "connectance" will be high. By analogical connectance we here mean that we have adapted Ashby's "connectance" concept to organisations. An important difference between Ashby's "connectance" concept and analogical "connectance" as used here, is that in social systems there will not be an immediateness in the connection between the elements, variables, and the actors, as assumed in Ashby's investigation, in addition to the interactions being circular, while Ashby's "connectance" concept was from linear systems.

Fig. 3 Structure of the flow of information in our thought experiment

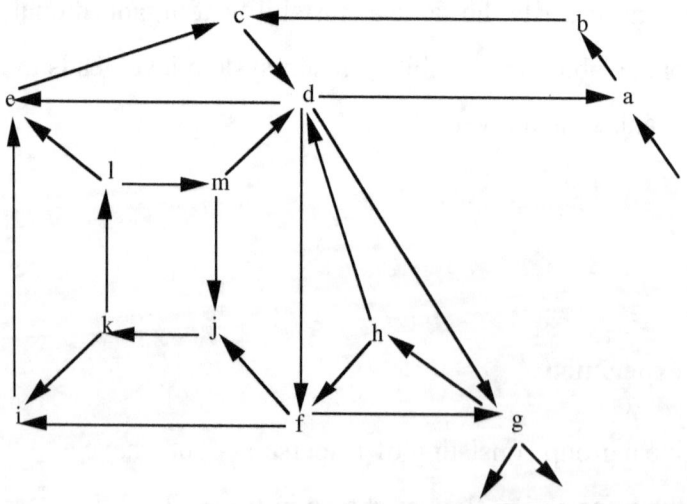

If we use our analogical "connectance" principle, the system modelled in fig. 3 is characterised by low stability (compare fig. 2). When the organisational channel capacity is large, we have previously contended that the potential for generation and spreading of ideas is large, certain things provided (compare part 3 of the chapter). If we further in our thought experiment presuppose that the working procedures of the group are based on complementary relationships, this will release the innovation potential, according to our previous argumentation.

The model shown in fig. 3 represents a group of 13 persons in an organisation. This group we imagine to be in charge of 19 critical functions mentioned by Miller (1978) in his theory of living systems at the organisational level. We further imagine that there are 19 such groups in the organisation. This is just one of many group selections we could have made. The point we are to reach, instability at sub-system level and stability at organisational level, will be equally well taken care of with e.g. 3, 4, or 5 groups.

We now link another piece of knowledge from Ashby to our thought experiment: If, says Ashby (1981:232), there in a system exists n- variables, and each variable can have a certain number of values (v), then the number of possible states on the relations are 2 squared in v squared in n. When a variable (n) assumes a certain value (v), it is one particular order which is determining for the relation, according to Ashby. An order of this kind reflects certain characteristics of the variable. If we say that a variable can only have two positions, i.e. upper and lower limit in an area of control, then we have reduced the complexity of the relations from Ashby's expression to 2 squared in 2 squared in n. If we further say that the variables of interest are the essential variables (e), i.e. those with crucial impact on the survival of the system, then the complexity of the relation is further reduced to 2 squared in 2 squared in e. The complexity is reduced because the essential variables are considerably smaller than the conceivable variables (n).

If we in our fictitious example say that the crucial functions (k) in a system can only have 2 essential variables under its surveillance, and there exist 19 K, which in our example constitute 19 groups, then every group keep control of the following conditions in the control area 2 squared in 2 squared in 2, which yields 16 states. If the total system, on the other hand, were to survey all conditions in our fictitious example, the relation would have been 2 squared in 2 squared in 38, which would be a very complex task, if at all possible.

What we so far have tried to show, is that the superior system cannot possible keep track of what is happening in the partial systems, even when the possibilities of variation are cut to the extreme extent as shown in our fictitious example. The consequences for organisational control of this thought experiment is that control must be left to those closest to the consequences of a decision. This also becomes obvious from the linking between "The Law of Requisite Variety" (Ashby, 1961) and "The Darkness Principle" (Clemson, 1984). Our thought experiment can also be regarded as an underlining of the importance of these two phenomena.

What we have tried to show in this thought experiment, is that instability at the subsystem level is a necessary condition for a high degree of innovation. Large channel capacity, and large analogical "connectance" gives unstable subsystems. If the goal is a high degree of innovation, we must accept instability at the sub-system level.

INSTABILITY AT THE SUB-SYSTEM LEVEL AND STABILITY AT THE TOTAL SYSTEM LEVEL

When the organisational channel capacity is large, the *frequency* of the flow of information is high, and the physical distance is small, the following phenomena occur in the organisation: The correction mechanism is built in prior to the behaviour, i.e. the organisation does not need to spend resources on central control, since the control of the partial systems is more or less self-correcting. The classic cybernetic regulation mechanism, with its feedback designs is incorporated as a part of the very communication process when the above-mentioned conditions are present. The feedback processes are not removed, but we are approaching the ideal state, where feedback is "instantaneous". The communicative density implies that errors do not have to be corrected for the future by controllers in the superior system. When the afore-mentioned conditions are present, the individual subsystems of the organisation will operate so that potential errors are corrected before they manifest themselves in physical action. Such a regulating mechanism being built in prior to the actual action, saves the organisation for human and financial resources for correction of manifested errors.

This also means that the superior systems do not have to locate or find the cause. What is needed is large organisational channel capacity, large analogical "connectance", and the placing of responsibility closest to the ones making the actual decision in the partial systems, namely the individual operators, in such a way that the consequences also weight on the individual operators decisions.

This indicates that instability at sub-system level, provided the occurrence of large organisational channel capacity and large analogical "connectance" leads to stability at the organisational level. A figurative presentation of our argumentation chain is made by Bateson (1972,1979), who often returns to his tight rope walker example. If, Bateson says, the tight rope walker is to remain stable on the tight rope, all partial systems (arms and legs) must be in constant change. Prigogine & Stenger (1984) argue in favour of the view that stability in a system is directly determined by the degree of communicative openness. This leads to their statement "order out of chaos". Chaos is the many interactions existing in the communicative process, and which are impossible to survey or control. But through this very communicative chaos emerges stability and order in the total system.

Fig.4 displays what we have tried to explain in the preceding thought experiment.

Fig.4 Stability presupposes instability

Analogical "Connectance"

	Large	Small
Large Organizational channel capacity	Instability at the sub-system level, and stability at the organizational level 1	Stability at the sub-system level, and stability at the organizational level 2
Small	Instability at the sub-system level, and rigidity at the organizational level 3	Stability at the sub-system level, and rigidity at the organizational level 4

It is only cell 1 which fulfils the condition of stability at the organisational level, and, at the same time a large innovation potential at the sub-system level, i.e. actor level. For the innovation potential to be released, it is required that the conditions treated in part 3 of the chapter are fulfilled.

CONCLUSION: MANAGERIAL IMPLICATIONS

A communication policy in organisations being based on :

open communication

free flow of information

the complementarity principle in the group, as a basis for communication, generation of ideas, and problem solving, will facilitate the following behaviour in organisations:

I. The re-creation of dialogue. In the dialogue free flow of ideas towards implemented targets for the organisation as a whole, can be developed. Dialogue is contrasted to discussion. In the discussion the struggle for the most potent arguments is in focus. In the dialogue it is permitted to ask "stupid questions", while the competition-related context itself to a very limited extent offers such an opportunity.

Turner (1990:74) makes the following statement about the open communicative environment: "Openness, even when not practised perfectly, encourages us to express our ideas and gives us access to ideas of others. It lets us know what is happening, why it is happening, and the thinking behind what is happening".

II. Holistic integration of information systems. It is possible to integrate the vertical, horizontal, and diagonal information structures of the organisation. This facilitates a view into, and more effective solutions to conflicts in the organisation. By integrating the various information structures, one also facilitates the construction of what Argyris (1990:8) says is lacking in organisations, namely: "Upward communication for difficult issues are often lacking".

III. Face-to face communication. This type of communication generates greater understanding of totality and knowledge of connections because of the interactive aspect. It is easier to get a view of the consequences of actions for other internal units of the organisation. A deeper understanding of decisions which are not necessarily beneficial for our own unit/department, is made possible. If the organisation has clear boundaries, both professionally and "geographically, the understanding of total relations is made difficult, and a competition for resources is often the outcome instead of co-operation in the exploitation of resources. It is the breadth of variation in terms of problem definition and problem solving which will be the interesting point in connection with behaviour characterised by the open communicative environment.

IV. Generation of an innovation environment. It is not so much new ideas within existing ways of thinking we need, but rather new ideas about how we think. The answer does not lie in amassing more and more knowledge inside an existing framework. What we ought to set the spotlight on is how we can transform data to information and information to knowledge.

On the individual level there can be internal principles for competing which have a tendency to strengthen fragmented knowledge- amassing, all this at the cost of a mutual support where one tries together to develop an understanding of the total situation.

Overcoming fragmentation must not be confused with, in the case of specific well defined problems, the fact that one ought to define and analyse in order to evaluate more closely causal series. It is, however when one defines and employs linear causal lines of thought related to conditions which are of non-linear nature that fragmentation must be overcome. In non-linear causality one should pay more attention to relationships, patterns, intertwined patterns and understanding of the total situation. When one isolates and analyses circular loops one breaks up patterns which are vital for understanding. It can be compared metaphorically with breaking a new laid egg to study the chick as it grows up.

A dynamic mutual relationship between the specialist and the generalist, between problem- definition and problem solution, between analysis and synthesis can seem to override the negative consequences of fragmentation. There are, however quibbling changes of power which push organisations into an emphasis on analysis and fragmentation.

Changes from analysis and specialist knowledge (which is of course necessary in some situations) to insight into complete organisational network structures, cybernetic thinking, circular causal relationships and communicative consciousness can be a creative factor for most organisations.

If such creative expansion does not take place, fragmentation will lead to a cumbersome organisation and internal struggles on the borders of the various system components. The organisation will therefore use a lot of its time and energy in finding solutions for such energy spills. If the worst comes to the worst they will use so many resources on inner problem solving and opportunistic behaviour that very little energy will be left for solving tasks that the organisation was originally designed to perform.

V. Development of communicative consciousness. The cybernetic situation (1) is here understood as the pre-conditions necessary for the development of communicative consciousness.
Communicative consciousness is an ideal demand on the communicating parties in analogy with Webers ideal demands on the bureaucratic organisation. Organisations are in this chapter looked upon as consisting of actors with a higher or lower degree of communicative consciousness. This view of organisations is to a great extent coincidental with Luhmann's view (1986). If the actors in an organisation develop a communicative consciousness it is our contention that the possibilities for increased innovation potential in the organisation to be developed.

Note

I. The ideal demands on the cybernetic situation, are:

1. The listener listens without evaluating the statements of others while he/she is speaking, i.e. the attention is focused on an asking, contrasted to an answer- oriented attitude.

2. The parties involved seek an open, free, and mutual dialogue, where the master/servant relationship is gone beyond completely.

3. The parties have complementarity as their starting point, i.e. supportive attitude, where unlimited trust is allowed to exist.

4. The actors possess the understanding that any explanation is subjective and fragmented.

5. The parties involved in the communicative process have the understanding that premises, suppositions, pre-conditions, and motives must be made explicit, and that the focus on moral/ethical results and consequences of organisational approaches and solutions to problems are self-evident entities.

6. The ability to see how your communicative actions affect the other party/parties in the dialogue.

7. Never to *use* other people to realise your own goals.

8. The only coercion that exists, is the obligation to explain by means of arguments your statements, and in this way validate the dialogue.

REFERENCES

Argyris, C. (1990)"Overcomming Organizational Defenses", Allyn & Bacon, London.

Ashby, W.R. (1961)"An Introduction to Cybernetics", Chapman & Hall LTD, New York.

Ashby, W.R. (1970)"Connectance of Large Dynamic (Cybernetic) Systems: Critical Values for Stability", Nature, Vol 228 no. 5273 Nov. 21, 1970.

Ashby, W.R. (1981)"Constraint Analysis of Many Dimentional Relations", In Conant, R. (Ed.) "Mechanisms of Intelligence",

Intersystems Seaside, California.

Bateson, G. (1972)"Steps to a Ecology of Mind", Intex Books, London.

Bateson, G. (1979)"Mind and Nature", (Swedish Translation, 1988, Symposium & Tryckeri, Stockholm.)

Burns, T. & Stalker, G.M.(1968) "The Management of Innovation", Tavistock, London.

Clemson, B. (1984)"Cybernetics: A New Management Tool", Abacus Press, Kent.

Hauan, A. & Johannessen, J-A. (1993) " Organizational Cybernetics", 1993, In Stowell, F.A., West, D. & Howell, J.G. "Systems Science: Addressing Global Issues" Plenum Press, New York.

Jarillo, I.C. (1988) "On Strategic Networks", Strategic Management Journal, 9: 31-41.

Johannessen, J-A.(1991)"The Holographic Organization: A Design Model", Cybenetics and Systems, 22: 41-55.

Johannessen, J-A. & Hauan, A. (1992)"Reaching out for Heterarchy: A Study of the Reorganization of a Norwegian Shipyard", Cybernetics and Systems, 23: 169-189.

Johannessen, J-A. & Hauan, A. (1993) "Communication a Systems Theoretical Point of View: Third Order Cybernetics" Systems Practice 1993.

Kanter, R. M. (1983)"The Change Masters", Unwin Hyman, London.

Khan, A.M. & Manopichetwattana, V. (1989) "Innovative and Non innovative Small Firms: Types and Characteristics", Management Science, 35, 5: 597-606.

Krehbiel, K. (1987)"Why are Congressional Committees Powerful?", American Political Science Review, 81: 929-935.

Luhman, N. (1986)"The Autopoiesis of Social Systems", In

Geyer, R.F. & Van der Zouwen, J. (eds.) "Sociocybernetic Paradoxes: Observation, Control and Evolution of Self-Steering.

MacMillan, I.C. (1983) "The Politics of New Venture Management", Harvard Business Review, 61, 6.

March, J.G. & Olsen, J.P. (1989) "Rediscovering Institutions: The Organizational Basis of Politics", Free Press, New York.

Miller,J.G. (1978)"Living Systems" , Mc Graw Hill, New York.

Prigogine, I. & Stenger, I. (1984)"Order out of Chaos: Mans New Dialogue with Nature" ,Bantam Books, Toronto.

Rogers, E.M. (1983) "Diffusion of Innovations", Free Press, New York.

Rogers, E.M.& Shoemaker,F. (1972)"The Communication of Innovations:A Cross-Cultural Approach", Free Press, Glencoe, Ill.

Rothwell, R.(1991) "External Networking and Innovation in Small and Medium-Sized Manufacturing Firms in Europe", Technovation, 11, 2: 93-112.

Shepsle, K. & Weingast, B.(1987) "Why are Congressional Commitees Powerful?", American Political Science Review. 81: 935-945.

Turner, C.H. (1990)"Charting the Corporate Mind: From Dilemma to Strategy", Basil Blackwel, London.

CHAPTER 2 CRITICAL INNOVATION FACTORS

Introduction

The systemic approach (see Bunge, 1983; 1985; 1989; 1992, Johannessen, 1996; 1997) to understanding innovation is more complex than linear models, but is, in our opinion, more realistic, than linear models. This is also stated by Soete & Arundel (1993: 29), Corcoran (1992), Rothwell (1992) and Frey (1989) etc. The systemic approach is in this chapter used interchangeable with the interactive model. The interactive model is in literature also referred to as the co-operation model and the cyclical model. The interactive model is used as a term, as it contrasts the linear model. The model must be understood as a starting point for a systemic approach, which in the event of repeated testing has to be altered. In cases of extensive research at the industry level the model has to be changed and refined in relation to the various industries.

It was not until the late 1980s that the systemic approach to the study of innovation and the practical application of these models gained acceptance. To get a full survey of the development, see Forrest (1991), Ziman (1991), Rothwell (1992), Lundval (1992).

The linear model is mainly based on formal knowledge (explicit knowledge) developed through R & D activities. The main hypotheses in this model is that: Extensive prioritising of R & D is closely related to extensive innovation degree. Policy implications of this thinking in the entire western world has been major emphasis on R & D activities in research and university environments. It is particularly basic research and technological knowledge which has been regarded as important. Smith (1994:2) says that this model is "research-based, sequential and technocratic". The linear model for innovation has been toned down, while more evolutionary economic theories (see Jacobsen, 1992) and new economic growth theories (see Verspagen 1992) have gained more acceptance. The limitations in the linear innovation model is the access to R & D resources internally in the company or thorough co-operation with other systems. The public policy is according to this model focused around various measures to increase R & D activities in the individual company, alone or in networks with others.

While the linear model focuses on explicit knowledge, the interactive model emphasises a system of relations between the following entities: R & D activities, structural links, tacit knowledge, interactive learning, the cultural context, social processes, national and regional innovation systems and customer and supplier relations (see Lundvall, 1992; Campagni, 1991:8).

It is the emphasis on a variety of knowledge types, and the links between them which is regarded as the most valuable resource in the interactive model, and interactive learning is regarded as the most important process (see Lundvall, 1992:9). Another dominant feature pertaining to the interactive innovation model is the store set by collaboration, as opposed to the emphasis on competition (see Lundvall & Johnson, 1994:26; You & Wilkinson, 1994;265).

The interactive innovation model observes the connection between organisational, technological, and environmental factors (see OECD, 1992; Smith, 1994; Klein & Rosenberg, 1986; Dosi, 1988; Malerba, 1992, Teece, 1989; Håkanson, 1989; Von Hippel, 1986). The model presupposes that innovation processes vary from company to company, and that there is a pattern of interactive processes which generates innovation activity in the individual companies.

The interactive model is based on theoretical assumptions for a more evolutionary economic theory (see Jacobsen 1992; Matcalfe, 1995:25-46) and knowledge derived from new economic growth theories (see Scott, 1989). In the interactive model R & D activities are not seen as the primary process generating innovations, but rather as part of a bigger system of relations among various elements: market contact, design, financial opportunities, the possibilities of linking the company to external knowledge systems, the use of information and communication technology, management skills, company culture, network activities and the regional and national innovation system (see Smith, 1994: 7-8; Klein & Rosenberg, 1986).

Schumpeter's view of the conditions for developing innovation changed from a very early view (Schumpeter, 1934) of the entrepreneur as the motor of innovation processes, to a later notion (Schumpeter, 1942), where he strongly emphasised the collective process constituted by the R & D activities. Through the concept national innovation systems, Lundvall (1988; 1992) and Nelson (1993), among others, further developed Schumpeter's view of innovation as an interactive process. It is the company-internal, company-external and national and regional innovation systems working in an interactive learning process which will constitute our focus of attention.

We will in this chapter look at the following question: What patterns of critical innovation factors promote/hinder innovation activity, seen from the individual company?

If we manage to answer this question adequately, we will have made a slight contribution to the understanding of growth and innovation processes at the company level.

The chapter is organised as follow: First we develop a conceptual model for organisational innovation. Then we discuss each element in the model. In the conclusion we interpret some research policy implications of the organizational innovation model.

Innovation as interactive learning: Developing a model

There are strong research indications that it is particularly innovation activities which can provide both newly established and formerly established companies with a greater survival capacity and also potential growth. This is also evident in the following quotation from the European Commission: " economic performance depends upon the progressive introduction over time of innovations in products and processes---" (European Commission, 1991). Innovation is increasingly seen as a considerable factor explaining economic growth in general, and as a competitive advantage as well as a condition for the survival of the company. This notion is clearly in evidence in the European Commission Green chapter on innovation (1995), in addition to OECD (1992).

A large number of international case studies have pointed out the connection between innovation and the competitive ability on the part of companies (see Freeman, 1982; Dosi, 1984; OECD, 1984). We will not argue in favour of these connections in this chapter, but regard the statement that economic growth and competitive ability presuppose continuous and radical innovations as a postulate (see Scott, 1989; Verspagen, 1992).

Innovation is here defined as "any idea, practice or material artefact perceived to be new by the relevant unit of adoption (Zaltman et. al. 1973). With this definition of innovation there is a distinction between innovation and change. All innovation presupposes change, but not all change presupposes innovation.

Innovation literature can be categorised as belonging to four different schools:

1. The individual-oriented.

2. The structure-oriented

3. The interactive

4. National and regional systems of innovation

The individual-oriented perspective emphasises concepts like: age, educational level, personal features, sex, cognitive style and creativity (see Scott & Bruce, 1994). Influential theoretical sources are here mainly the rational actor and the limited rationality (see Pettigrew, 1985:20: Cyert & March, 1963: 278).

The structural perspective focuses on organisational characteristics. Influential theoretical sources here are structural functionalism, system theory and contingency theory. A strongly emphasised area in this perspective is the relationship between the organisation and the environment (see Slappendal, 1996: 113 - 118).

The interactive perspective has recently received a lot more attention (see Van de Ven, etc., 1989; Van de Ven & Rogers, 1988). The emphasis in this perspective is the focus on dynamic changes over a period of time. The focus in this perspective is on how an action influences structure over a period of time, and vice versa, in the innovation process (see Van de Ven & Poole, 1988). Furthermore importance has been attached to the political context in the interactive perspective (see Child & Smith, 1987). It is methodically longitudinal studies which are sought after in this perspective (see Pettigrew, 1985; 1987; Walton, 1987), whereas it is mainly statistical analyses which have been used in the other two.

A fourth research school increasingly focused on in recent years, is the study on how national and regional innovation systems influence innovation activity in companies (see Nelson & Winter. 1982; Lundvall & Johnson, 1994). Focus in this school is on the organisation and distribution of knowledge. It is the cognitive infrastructure and the organisation of networks between knowledge institutions and companies which are emphasised in particular in this perspective.

Successful innovations presuppose external orientation on the part of the companies (see Dodgeson, 1993). In Norway Smith and Vidvei (1992), among others, have pointed to the relationship between innovation activity and external orientation towards the client/customer, suppliers, and the university/college sector. The main motives from companies to engage in the collaboration and external systems, as reported by Smith and Vidvei, are, among other things, incomplete internal competence, the wish for cost reductions, and the desire to reduce the time devoted to developing new products. The main focus for Norwegian companies is the wish for improved competence through external orientation. The highest rewards of eternal orientation as far as Norwegian companies are concerned, have been reported to be the access to external competence, the learning effect for one's own employees and expanded knowledge of existing technology (Smith & Vidvei, 1992). The same survey also reports that companies having external R & D collaboration, also have the by far largest share of new products in their portfolio. The tendency is further reinforced for companies linked to R & D co-operation with foreign research institutes. The link to R & D institutions has also proved to be closely related to ROI, productivity and increased export (see Freeman, 1987).

There are mainly four approaches which have received attention, in terms of innovation and external sources. These are customer - supplier relations (see Von Hippel, 1989), network studies (see Håkanson, 1989, Midley et al. 1992); market conditions (see Ames & Hlavacek, 1988; Ancona & Caldwell, 1992) and national and regional innovation systems (see Lundvall, 1992; Nelson, 1993).

Several studies have pointed out certain internal factors as critical for the innovation potential in companies. The most critical innovation factors appears to be: cultural factors (see Hage & Dewar, 1973); structural links, i.e. information, communication and learning processes (see Teece, 1986; 1988 Tushman & Nadler, 1986); internal competence (see Drucker, 1985; Quinn, 1992); The role of management (see Howell & Higgins, 1990); and the importance of information and communication technology (ICT) (see Freeman, 1991; Antonelli, 1993).

The picture emerging from several studies appears to underline the picture of a multitude of factors interacting in order to induce innovation in economic life. We have grouped these main entities in the following way: Company internal factors, company external factors and national and regional innovation systems.

Figure 1 Innovation as interactive learning

```
                    ┌─────────────────────────────────────┐
                    │  Company internal factors           │
                    │  Culture                            │
                    │  Structural links                   │
                    │  Competence                         │
                    │  Management                         │
                    │  Information and communication technology │
                    └─────────────────────────────────────┘
                                    │ determines
                                    ▼
                         ┌──────────────────────┐
   Influence and is      │  Organizational      │    Influence and is
   influenced by         │  innovation          │    influenced by
                         └──────────────────────┘
                           ▲              ▲
                determines │              │ determines
   ┌─────────────────────┐                ┌─────────────────────┐
   │ National and regional│ Influence and │ Company external    │
   │ innovation systems   │ is influenced │ factors             │
   │                      │ by            │                     │
   │                      │◄─────────────►│ Customer and        │
   │                      │               │ supplier relations  │
   └─────────────────────┘                └─────────────────────┘
```

In the remainder of the chapter we will discuss each of the critical innovation factors suggested by the model as determining for innovation.

Company-internal factors

Culture

By culture is here meant the value system expressed by an organisation (company) explicitly or implicitly (se Bunge, 1989). The company's value system is supposed to have a strong impact on innovation activities (see Hage & Dewar, 1973:281). The value system of a company also has a determining effect on learning processes and thus both the development of competence and the use of information from external sources, which has turned out to have great importance for innovation activities (Rogers, 1983; Rothwell, 1991; MacMillan, 1983).

Mansfield etc. (1981) discovered that about 60% of potentially successful innovations were copied within five years. At the same time costs for companies performing the copying were 35% lower than for companies having developed the innovation. The study of Levin et. al., (1987) underlines Mansfield's finding, and further indicates that non-patented innovations are often copied within one year. An important point of reporting these findings is that companies must focus on "invisible assets", tacit knowledge and context-confidence on the part of the actors, as these entities are of a type not susceptible to being copied by others. It is the invisible factors, which also constitute the culture of a company (see Barney, 1986). It is also these factors, according to Reed & DeFillippi (1990) and Winter (1987), which probably will have the greatest impact on company performance level. The discussion regarding the emphasis on the observable versus the unobservable factors in the study of innovation and economic growth, also signifies a boundary between the neo-classical and the "Austrian School" in economic theory (see Kirtzner, 1976; Itami & Roehl, 1987; Bonama, 1985). The invisible advantages are important to grasp in innovation research, as they represent advantages not easily copied by the competitors, and are directly linked to the internal culture in the company. This is also linked to the discussion around incremental and radical-innovations. Too much emphasis on R & D activities in order to elicit radical innovations and thus competitive edges, will put the company in a competitive situation. But, only until the competitors has copied the product or the process. Then the equilibrium in the competitive situation will be restored. More emphasis on incremental-innovations, or continuous change may constantly destabilise the market and be of significant value for the companies in terms of competitive advantage (see Mansfield, 1988; 1988a).

Structural links

Structural links are directly linked to information and communication processes, internally in the company and between the company and the surroundings. It is "searching/exploring" activities which are in focus in the construct structural links. The construct is closely linked to Ashby's (1970) concept "connectance" (see Johannessen, 1993:249-263).

Ashby (1970) asked the following question in an chapter in "Nature": If a large system is assembled (connected) at random, or has grown haphazardly, should we expect it to be stable or unstable? And how does the expectation change as n, the number of variables, tends to infinity? Ashby in this chapter points to the high probability for the stability to decrease as the variables increase, and possibly as quickly as 2 squared in minus n. The results pointed out by Ashby were from linear systems which were 100% connected, i.e. that changes in one variable has an immediate effect on the other variable.

Ashby in this chapter introduces the concept "connectance" (structural links), which is the degree of connectance in percent, i.e. if a change in one variable has an immediate effect on the other variables, connectance is 100%. If the change in one variable does not have any effect on the other variables, connectance is 0%. Connectance thus varies between 0 and 100%. If connectance is 10, this means that the change in one variables has an immediate effect on the 10 percent of the other variables in the system. By using this analogy to social systems, which are rarely linear, we manage to relate structural links directly to a company's learning processes.

The importance of interactive learning in companies for innovation processes has been discussed by Teece (1986; 1988), among others. Tushman & Nadler (1986: 75) explicitly express that innovative organisations have one thing in common. They are : "highly effective learning systems". In order to achieve this, the authors say, the organisations are required to display the ability for "both stability and change (1986:75). Understood in this way structural links are a very robust empirical indicators of company performance and innovative ability (see Clark & Fujimoto, 1991; Dougherty, 1992; Zirger & Maidique, 1990). These authors discuss the internal structural links in organisations, particularly cross-functional teams, and how they affect performance and innovation ability. Good internal structural links in organisations have turned out to be critical for the development of successful innovations (see Freeman, 1982; 1987a, Womack et al, 1990).

Several authors argue that an open communicative environment and a free flow of information promotes innovation processes in organisations. Among these authors we can mention Rogers & Shoemaker (1971), Kanter (1983), Rotwell (1991), Rogers (1983), Jarillo (1988) and MacMillan (1983). In such contexts actors find it easier to get in touch with others, both for support and for criticism of personal opinions. They will also in a more direct way be able to use other people's special knowledge. In this borderline area between several types of expertise, innovations will have the facility to grow. Furthermore in such an environment the link between theory and practice will more easily be established. In such a meeting practical experience and theoretical insight will more easily support the organisation as a whole.

A precondition for this development is that the organisation develops a communication policy, furthering complementary relations, i.e. relations where basic trust is in evidence, and where a helping and supportive attitude constitutes the foundation (Johannessen, 1995: Johannessen & Hauan, 1994).

The open communicative environment is further based on the assumption that communication can be carried out vertically, horizontally, as well as diagonally in the organisation. In addition there should be open lines of communication to the environment, with the exception of information which is sensitive to the organisation.

Several studies show that the degree of innovation in organisations emphasising written communication is less than in organisations which promote face-to-face communication (Kanter, 1983; Burns & Stalker,

1966). The explanation to this fact could be the fact that expediency in spreading ideas, immediate feed-back and correction can take place more easily in face-to-face communication than through formal written procedures. Kanter (1983:189) makes the following explicit statements: "Open communication serves a very important function for the potential innovator".

An open communicative environment based on relationships where trust and a helping basic attitude prevails (complementary relations), ensures that information is not used in a scramble for strategic positions for the purpose of serving personal interests at the expense of interests pertaining to the total system. Examples in literature of information games, where the actors use information in order to serve their own personal interests at the expense of the total interests of the organisation, can be found with Krehbiel (1987), Shepsle & Weingast (1987) and March & Olsen (1989).

Competence

Competence build-up in companies is essential in an innovation context for at least two reasons. High internal competence is important for the development of internal innovative solutions. But perhaps more important is the fact that high internal competence is often a prerequisite to utilise the diffusion of information and technology in the environment.

High internal competence functions metaphorically as a map, from which the company can find its paths around the environment. The better the map, the greater the probability for the company to be able to use different innovations.

Many SMC will not be in the position to maintain high internal competence in areas where this is recommended from an innovation point of view. This is an important premise for the understanding of the linking in networks, and links between companies and the national and regional innovation systems. For a discussion about SMC and the transfer of technology, see Nooteboom et al (1992).

As far as the companies are concerned, their specific competence in their field is mentioned as an attempt to explain why some companies are slight front-runners in the scramble for customers. Some regard competence as the most decisive competitive factor in the future, even as far as survival is concerned (Drucker, 1985; Quinn, 1992, Nonaka & Takeuchi, 1995; Barton, 1995).

Knowledge is gradually more accessible for companies through purchases, strategic alliances, network exchange, electronic networks and trough scientific periodicals. Competitive advantages based on knowledge thus provide an increasingly short-lived leg up. Therefore knowledge will have to be transformed into competence in conducive to copying, according to Prahlad and Hamel (1990). Nonaka & Takeuchi (1995) underline this even more by focusing on the importance of tacit knowledge for the development of continuous innovations in economic life in Japan.

Similar to other resources, like e.g. capital and work, competence has certain qualities. Competence is a resource which may be in conducive to division in smaller units. This is due to its being primarily linked to persons. Competence also has clear limitations with regards to time.

Furthermore it is not easily convertible or negotiable. One of the most critical aspects of competence-generative efforts, will in other words be the degree in which it is practicable to transfer the competence to a real work situation. Competence can be too general or specific. General competence can be negotiated in the labour market generally, whereas specific competence can only be exploited in the individual companies.

Knowledge is regarded as the most critical element in the competence concept, but knowledge has no intrinsic value alone. For knowledge to be instrumental in the generation of values, application to a task by persons possessing certain skills would be a requirement. Competence also implies a link between knowledge, tasks, and skills. By using this view as one's basis, the company's various fields of competence will be represented through the knowledge of the company (the knowledge system), tasks performed by the company (the task system) and available skills (the skill system) of the persons belonging to the organisation. The link between these entities will constitute the competence area of the company, i.e. the value-generating competence potential.

Management

In the literature's it is commonly accepted that innovative activities are promoted by "champions" (see Howell & Higgins, 1990). These are persons taking charge and burning to carry out ideas. A leader could be a "champion" of this kind or he/she can introduce new ideas through his external information and communication activities. The leader can also indirectly further innovation through clear visions, the reward system, strategy formation, in addition to goals and the result system (see

Iwamura & Jog, 1991).

How the management acts in the face of innovation is critical for the results to be expected. If the management is not innovation-oriented, focus in the entire organisation will be on here and now results, status quo and daily problem solutions. Tushman & Nadler (1986:92) explicitly state about the relationship between management and innovation: " there is perhaps no more pressing managerial problem than the sustained management of innovation, there is nothing mysterious about innovation; it don't just happen. Rather, it is the calculated outcome of strategic management and visionary leadership that provide people, structures, values and learning opportunities to make it an organisational way of life".

If the management is reluctant to be innovative, it is little other members of the company can do to generate an acceleration effective innovative policy, according to Rothwell (1977). Successful innovations are also linked to an open style of leadership, something that can be reinforced by the use of communication-related IT.

Kanter (1983) argues that the management must persuade rather than request, and it is necessary to recognise the competence of those who are underneath the management to generate positive changes. Increased education also leads to demands for autonomy, flexibility and freedom. This will generate new types of management and threaten old authorities, according to Kanter (1983).

In a study of innovative companies Quinn (1985) found, among other things, that innovation was generated continuously as the management would be actively involved in the innovation process, while leading values system and atmosphere of the company in a fashion conducive to innovations.

Maybe the biggest problem of managing complex organisations today, and innovation in particular, is the management of the partial/total relation, according to Van de Ven (1986). Van de Ven proposes the use of the holography metaphor in order to design the innovation process, so that the more of the totality is structured into each of the parts. Van de Ven suggests four holographic principles to manage the part/total relation:

1. Self-organising groups

2. Sufficient variation

3. Redundant functions.

4. Relatively little time lags.

The holographic principle for developing innovative ideas will depend on the generation of an institutional context, breeding innovation. The self-organising units must also be coupled closely to the organisational learning system, ensuring that knowledge integration is secured throughout the organisation. The flexible management practice is necessary for the development of innovations, and often entail problems for the established culture of companies. Managers can permit "chaos" or structural plurality in the early phase of an innovation process. This will, however, require more normal planning and control as the cost-incurring development unfolds (see Quinn, 1985).

Information and communication technology (ICT)

Information technology is here defined as (Scott Morton, 1991) a group of different elements consisting of:

1. Hardware

2. Software

3. Tele-communication networks

4. Work stations

5. Robots

6. Intelligent parts (chips)

Information and communication technology is an important prerequisite for innovation processes in companies today. The access to information and the opportunities to develop networks are facilitated as a result of this technology. One important point is, however, that the structure and organisation of the company can inhibit the use of information and communication technology in an innovation context. ICT has also in several studies turned out to have a major impact on innovative success (see e.g. Freeman, 1991; Antonelli, 1993).

There appears to be four research trends around IT and organisational change processes (Rockart & Short, 1988) which have been dominating. These are:

1. Information technology and the effect on organisational structure, including roles, power,

and restructuring.

2. Information technology and its effect on co-operation in organisations.

3. Information technology and cost reduction

4. Information technology and organisational integration processes.

From the beginning of the 1980s, there has been major focus on IT and increased organisational efficiency. In literature this focus has most often been linked to increased internationalisation, increased market risk, cost, reductions, increased productivity and more intimate relations between the customer and the company (Hammer & Champy, 1993).

At the end of the 1980s and the beginning of the 1990s, the focus has been more centred on entities such as IT and competitive edges, IT and strategic potential, IT and innovation, IT and communication, IT and network organisations and particularly IT and customer service. "MIT Sloan School of management" has since 1984 been working on the research program "The Management in the 1990s". Six important results from this project are (Scott Morton, 1991):

1) IT facilitates fundamental changes in work methods

2) IT facilitates integration of company functions at all levels and between organisations.

3) IT implies changes in the competitive climate in many industries.

4) IT generated new strategic possibilities for organisations.

5) Successful application of IT will require changes in management

philosophy and organisational structure:

6)An important challenge for management philosophy in the 1990s will be to lead organisations through the transformation which is necessary to achieve progress in the global environment.

IT makes it possible to integrate learning about complex group interactions and thus promote creativity and innovation. Technology also makes reflection, disclosure, testing, and improvement of mental models used as support when being faced with difficult problems, possible. It offers the opportunity for organisational learning through various types of simulation tools and interactive activities. Dynamic and complex business relations can thus be investigated through the testing of strategies and procedures through dynamic modelling tools, and the analysis of possible consequences and various change strategies, according to Senge (1991). With the information technology today, the working life of goods and services will be shortened considerably in many types of business. This will have bearing on the design and innovation frequency of the products. Morgan (1989) thinks that it might be an idea to develop products which can be changed through swapping old component with new ones, or by replacing one electronic chip with a new one, which would increase the degree of innovation and durability for the core product, but generate innovatively new commercial products.

Company-external factors

Customer and supplier relations

The connection between customer closeness and innovation was focused on in the 1960s and 1970s through demand-led theories. Myers & Marquis' (1969) study of more than 500 innovative companies confirmed the importance of customer relations for innovation activities in companies. The same phenomenon is confirmed by Mowery & Rosenberg (1982: 193-241). This connection is strongly emphasised by Andersen (1994:47-55) as an important source of innovation. Andersen points to the fact that it is the interactive learning process happening in a borderline area, which has a releasing effect on innovation activities. Andersen (1994:57) explicitly expresses: "--firms with well-established information channels to sophisticated customers have a comparative advantage in the creation of minor innovations."

Through customer closeness not only incremental-innovations are developed. Just as important are continuos incremental-innovations, resulting from customer closeness. Lundvall (1988) strongly emphasises the "user-producer" closeness and argues in favour of this being a "learning by interacting" process promoting innovation. Both Rosenberg (1982) and Arrow (1962) have made suggestions to the same effect with their respective concepts "learning by using" and "learning by doing".

There will usually be a link between customer closeness, market sensitivity, and technology push, setting off innovative processes in companies (see Midley et. al, 1992, Deshpande et. al, 1993). Customer orientation is meant to generate values for customers (Porter, 1985). At the same time close customer relations are a way of knowing which innovations have the capacity for success. The first ones to empirically test the relationship between customer orientation and company performance were Narver & Slater (1990). Their findings concluded that there is a positive connection between customer orientation and earning. The study of Despande et al. (1993) supported Narver & Slater's study, while bringing evidence of greater innovative activity and increased customer closeness. Customer orientation is also closely linked to the company having accurate information about the market. Customer orientation must therefor meet two different demands. Companies must be sensitive to customer wishes, while always being a leg up in relation to the competition. Innovation will thus be a means to secure that these demands are met (see Ames & Hlavacek, 1988; Day, 1990). Customers affect the innovative processes through their wishes, needs and idea material (see Utterback, 1982; Von Hippel, 1988; Muntel & Merdith, 1986). In company literature there has been extensive focus on stressing customer satisfaction and customer loyalty. Customer loyalty in an innovation context is however a double-edged sword. On the one hand loyalty is positive for the individual company, but if the loyalty is too great, it can easily lead to a weakening of general alertness toward competitor behaviour, which could have serious consequences. In an innovation context customer satisfaction is thus a positive concept, whereas customer loyalty is a more questionable entity. Customers will easily switch to a competing company if the innovation ability is not optimal in the company in question. Potential disloyalty from the customers can thus be seen as an impetus in the innovation process. Companies stressing and achieving a high degree of customer loyalty can thus in a subtle way be very fragile in relation to companies with a well-developed innovation strategy, where customer closeness, not customer loyalty is emphasised.

National and regional innovation systems

The first one to explicitly use the term national innovation system was Freeman (1987a). Also Nelson's study (1987; 1988) focused on this phenomenon. Then the term was developed by Lundvall (1988; 1992), Andersen & Lundvall (1988) and Johnson & Lundvall (1991). Porter's (1990) contribution could be seen in the same light. The idea of national innovation systems could in fact be traced back to List's idea of national systems for political economy, according to Freeman (1995:5). The main idea in List's system is protection of new growing industries, technology, skills and the application of them. For the national innovation system the importance of investing in the knowledge-related infrastructure, not just the physical infrastructure, is being stressed. This has, among other things, been discussed by the World Bank (1991) and OECD (1992). The OECD report underlines, among other things, that:

1. There is a 30-40- year time lag, with regards to fundamental research and radical

    innovations

2. There is a 4-5 -year time lag with regards to applied research and incremental innovations.

The OECD report (1992:39) further emphasises that the critical factor to achieve success and innovation is the link between technological knowledge accumulation, company-internal learning processes and institutional strength.

The capital concept is the essential element in the discussion about national innovation systems. It is however more interesting to observe the knowledge capital being invested in the individual knowledge systems and in the network between knowledge institutions, than the classic concept of capital. The idea is that innovative success for the individual companies will depend on the existing national knowledge capital. Variables which often appear as important in relation to national innovation systems are the following:

The public support framework

National financing systems (bank, insurance etc.)

R & D environments

Technical/economic competence

Organisational competence

International contacts

The idea of intellectual capital being important for a nation's political economy is not new. Even List in his polemic against the teachings of Adam Smith, underlines the importance of this point quite strongly. There are, however, types of cultural links between the knowledge capital and companies which are interesting due to the extensive focus on national innovation systems. The various nations are very diverse in terms of tradition regarding this link, and this is reflected in the view on the part of companies of the necessity to maintain close relations between the various knowledge system and the companies (see OECD, 1992, European Commissions, 1995). The idea of knowledge as a determining factor for innovation and growth has not been paid due attention to by neo-classic economy, but is mainly ingrained in what roughly could be described as the Austrian school (see Jacobsen, 1992).

The idea of national innovation systems focuses on strategic measures directed towards the knowledge infrastructure. These are regarded as important elements for innovation processes and economic growth. It is not the development of specific technologies and products which the constructs national and regional innovation systems are concerned about (see Lundvall, 1988;1992; Mc Elvery, 1991), but the structural links between the knowledge capital and the companies. The connection between the companies and knowledge capital must further be linked towards a network of international knowledge institutions for the most efficient promotion of innovation potential in the individual companies.

It is the systemic nature which is focused on in national and regional innovation systems, not the analysis or focus on one or more elements constituting the concepts. This appears quite clearly from OECD (1992:2): "National system of innovation involve a set of networks linked in such a way that the creation and diffusion of technology and its transformation into commercial products depends as much on the vitality of the whole set of relationships as on the individual performance of any given element of the system". The systemic nature of the national and regional innovation system means that the focus both on research and policy implications must be on the system of relations, and how these relations should be coupled structurally.

It would not be sufficient to strengthen the regional innovation system by means of financial and technological support. The strong turbulence and innovation in the market and in technology requires scanning systems and structural links which SMC are not in the position to get access to, neither in the initial phase nor later.

Conclusion

Innovation is supposed to be a major element in economic growth, and secure an improved competitive position for the companies. Innovation research is a fundamental study of change processes, knowledge development and knowledge integration, for the purpose of generating new combinations. To uncover critical innovation factors hindering/promoting change processes, knowledge development and knowledge integration is thus regarded as essential in innovation research. Knowledge is to a great extent a result of interactive learning processes at various system levels. How these learning processes can be improved is thus essential for innovation.

The research policy implications of the interactive model will be that the emphasis on research must turn more toward relations between elements generating innovation systems at various system levels, in order to disclose patterns hindering/promoting innovation in social systems, i.e. a systemic research perspective. To achieve this goal several methods must be applied in the same research project or at least research program, e.g. statistical investigations, hypothesis testing, longitudinal studies, comparative studies and more angles of incidence based on action research. By using an interdisciplinary approach simultaneously, we may find ourselves in a position to disclose the system of relations between elements constituting the pattern which hinders/promotes innovation.

REFERENCES

Ames, B.C. & J.D. Hlavacek (1988). Market driven Management: Prescription for survival in a turbulent world, Irwin Homewood.

Ancona, D.G. & D.F. Caldwell (1992). Bridging the boundary: External process and performance in organization teams, Administrative Science Quarterly, 37: 634-665.

Andersen, E.S. (1994). Evolutionary Economics: Post-Schumperterian Contributions, Pinter, London.

Andersen, E.S. & Lundvall, B-Å. (1988). Small National Systems of Innovation Facing Technological Revolutions-An Interpretive Framework. In Freeman, C. & Lundvall, B-Å. (eds.). Small countries facing the technological revolution, Pinter, London.

Antonelli, C. (1993). The dynamics of technological interrelatedness: the case of information and communication technologies. I D. Foray & C. Freeman (red.). Technology and the wealth of nations, Pinter, London.

Arrow, K.J. (1962). The Economic implications of Learning by Doing, Review of Economic Studies, Vol. xxix, no. 80

Ashby, W.R. (1970)"Connectance of Large Dynamic (Cybernetic) Systems: Critical Values for Stability" Nature, Vol 228 no. 5273 Nov. 21, 1970

Barney, J. (1986). Organizational Culture: Can it be a source of sustained competitive advantage? Academent of Management Review, 11: 656-665.

Bonoma, T.V. (1985). Case research in marketing: Opportunities, problems, and a process, Journal of marketing Research, 22: 199-208.

Bunge, M.(1983). Exploring the World. Dordrecht: Reidel.

Bunge, M. (1985). Philosophy of Science and Technology. Part I. Dordrecht: Reidel.

Bunge, M. (1989). Ethics: The Good and the Right, Reidel, Dordrecht.

Bunge, M. (1992). Systems Everywhere, In Negoita, C.V. (ed.), Cybernetics and Applied Systems,pp. 23-43, Marcell Deker, New York.

Burns, T. & Stalker, M. (1966). The management of innovation, Tavistock Publication, London.

Camagni, R. (red.). (1991). Innovation networks: spatial perspective, Belhaven Press, London.

Child, J. & C.Smith (1987). The context and process of organizational transformation, Journal of Management Studies, 24: 565-593.

Clark, K.B. & T. Fujimoto (1991). Product development performance, Harvard Business School Press, Boston.

Corcoran, E. (1992). Redesigning research, Scientific American: 72-80 june.

Cyert, R. M. & J.G. March (1963). A Behavioral Theory of the Firm, Prentice Hall, Englewood Cliffs, NJ.

Day, G.S. (1990). Market driven strategy: Processes for creating value, Free Press, New York.

Deshpande, R., J.U. Farley & F.E. Webster jr. (1993). Corporate Culture, customer orientation and innovation in Japanese firms: A quadrad analysis, Journal of Marketing, 57, 1: 23-37.

Dodgson, E.M. (1993). Technological collaboration in industry, strategy, policy and internalisation in innovation, Oxford University Press, London.

Dosi, G. (1984). Technical Change and Industrial Transformation, Macmillan, London.

Dosi, G. (1988). Sources, procedures and microeconomic effect of innovation, Journal of Economic Litterature, Vol. 36: 1126-71.

Dougherty, D. (1992). Interpretive barriers to successful product innovation in large firms, Organization Science, 3: 179-202.

Drucker, P.F. (1985). Innovation and Entrepreneurship: Practic and Principles, Heineman, London.

European Commission (1991). Four Motors for Europe: An analysis of cross-regional cooperation, Fast Occasional Chapter no. 241, CEC, DG XII, Vol. 17.

European Commission, (1995). Green chapter on innovation, Brussel.

Forrest, J.E. (1991). Models of the process of technological innovation, Technology Analysis & Strategic Management, 3: 439-453.

Freeman, C. (1982). The Economics of Industrial Innovation, Pinter, London.

Freeman, C. (red.) (1987). Output Measurement in Science and Technology, North Holland, Amsterdam.

Freeman, C. (1987a). Technology Policy and Economic Performance: Lessons from Japan, Pinter, London.

Freeman, C. (1991). Networks of innovators: A synthesis of research issues, Research Policy, vol. 20, no. 5, 499-514.

Freeman, C. (1995). The National System of Innovation in historical Perspective, Cambridge Journal of Economics, 19: 5-24.

Frey, D.N. (1989). Junk your linear R&D, Research & Technology Management, 32: 7-8.

Hage, J. & R. Dewar (1973). Elite values versus organizational structure in predicting innovation, Administrative Science Quarterly, 18: 279-290.

Hammer, M and Champy, J. (1993). "Reengineering the Corporation", Harper Business, New York.

Håkanson, H. (1989).Corporate technological Behavior-Corporation and Networks, Pinter, London.

Itami, H. & T.W. Roehl (1987). Mobilizing invisible assets, Harvard University Press, Cambridge, MA.

Iwamura, A. & V.M. Jog (1991). Innovators, organization structure and management of the innovation process in the securities industry, Journal of Product Innovation Management, 8: 104-116.

Jacobsen, R. (1992). The Austian School of Strategy, Academy of Management Review, 17, 4: 782-807.

Jarillo, I.C. (1988). "On Strategic Networks", Strategic Management Journal, 9: 31-41.

Johannessen, J-A. (1993). Cybernetics and Innovation: The `Hopeless`choice between stability and innovation in Organizations, Entrepreneurship, Innovation and Change, Vol.2, No.3, 249-263.

Johannessen, J-A. (1996). "Systemics Applied to the Study of Organizational Fields: Developing a Systemic Research Strategy for Organizational Fields". Kybernetes, vol. 25, 1: 33-51.

Johannessen, J-A. (1997). Aspects of causal processes, Kybernetes, Vol. 26, nr. 1: 30-52.

Johannessen, J-A. (1995). "Basic Features of an Information and Communication System Aimed at Promoting Organizational Learning" Systems Practice, Vol. 8, No. 2: 183- 197.

Johannessen, J-A., Dolva, J-O., & Olsen, B. (1997). Organizing

Innovations, Integrating Knowledge Systems, European Planning Studies, 5;3:331-349.

Johannessen, J-A., Olaisen, J & Hauan, A. (1993). A Norwegian Shipyard Fasing the Russian Market, European Journal of Marketing, 3: 23-39.

Johannessen,J-A. & Hauan, A. (1994). "Communication. A System Theoretical Point of View","Systems Practice", 7, nr. 1:63-73, 1994.

Johannessen, J-A.; Olsen, B., & Olaisen, J. (1997). Process Organising: A Strategy for Continous Innovation and Limiting Imitation, Long Range Planning, 30,1: 96-110.

Johnson, B. & Lundvall, B-Å. (1991). Flexibility and institutional learning. In Jessop, B. et.al. The Politics of flexibility, Edward Elgar, Aldershot.

Kanter, R.M. (1983). "The Change Masters", Tuchstone, New York.

Kirzner, I.M. (1976). On the method of Austrian economics. I E.G. Dolan (red.). The foundation of modern Austrian economics, 40-51, Sheed & Ward, Kansas City, MO.

Klein, S. & Rosenberg, N. (1986). An Overview of innovation. I R.Landan & N. Rosenberg (red.). The positive sum strategy, National Academy Press, Washington.

Krehbiel, K. (1987)"Why are Congressional Committees Powerful?",

American Political Science Review, 81: 929-935.

Levin, R.C., A.K. Klevorik, R.R. Nelson & S.G.Winter (1987).

Appropriating the returns from industrial research and development, Brookings chapters on Economic Activity: 783-820.

Lundvall, B.Å. (1988). Innovation as an interactive process from User-producer interaction to the national system of innovation, I G. Dosi, C.Freeman, R.Nelson, G. Silverberg & L. Soete (red.),349-370. Technical Change and Economic Theory, Pinter, London.

Lundvall, B.Å. (red.). (1992). National Systems of Innovation, Pinter, London.

Lundvall, B.Å. & B.Johnson (1994). The Learning economy, Journal of industry studies, 1, 2: 23-42.

Malerba, F. (1992). The Organization of the innovative process. I N. Rosenberg; R. Landan & D. Mowery (red.). Technology and the Wealth of Nations, s. 247-280, Stanford University Press, Stanford.

March, J.G. & Olsen, J.P. (1989) "Rediscovering Institutions: The Organizational Basis of Politics", Free Press, New York.

MacMillan, I.C. (1983). The politics of new venture management, Harvard Business Review, nov./des., 61,6.

Mansfield, E. (1988). Industrial R&D in Japan and the United States: A Comparative study, American Economic Review Chapters and Proceedings, 78: 223-228.

Mansfield, E. (1988a). The speed and cost of industrial innovation in Japan and the United States: External vs. internal innovations, Management Science, 34: 1157-1168.

Mansfield, E., M. Schwartz & S. Wagner (1981). Imitation costs and patents: An empirical study, Economic Journal, 91: 907-918.

Mantel, S.J. & J.R. Meredith (1986). The role of customer cooperation in the development, marketing and implementation of innovations. I H. Hubner (red.). 27-36, Tke Art and Science of Innovation management, Elsevier science, Amsterdam.

McElvey, M. (1991). How do national systems of innovation differ. I G. Hodgson og E. Screpanti (red.) Rethinking Economics, Edward Elgar, Aldershot.

Metcalfe, J.S. (1995). Technology systems and technology policy in an evolutionary framework, Cambridge Journal of Economics, 19: 25-46.

Midley, D.F., P.D. Morrison & J.H. Roberts (1992). The effect of network structure in industrial diffusion processes, Research Policy, vol 21, no. 6: 533-552.

Mowery, D. & Rosenberg, N. (1979). The Influence of Market Demand upon innovation: A critical review of some recent empirical studies, Research Policy, Vol. 8, no.2.

Myers, S. & D.G. Marquis (1969). Successful industrial innovation, National Science Foundation, Washington.

Nelson, R.R. (1987). Understanding Technical Change as an Evolutionary Process, North-Holland, Amsterdam.

Nelson, R.R. (1988). Institutions supporting technical change in the United States. I G. Dosi, C.Freeman, R.Nelson, G. Silverberg & L. Soete (red.),349-370. Technical Change and Economic Theory, Pinter,

London.

Nelson, R. R. (red.). (1993). National Innovation Systems, Oxford University Press, Oxford.

Nelson, R.R. & S.G. Winter (1982). An Evolutionary Theory of Economic Change, Harvard University Press, Cambridge, Mass.

Nonaka, I. & Takeuchi, H. (1996). The Knowledge Creating Company, Oxford University Press, Oxford.

Nooteboom, B., C. Coehoorn & A.D. Van der Zwaan (1992). The purpose and effectiveness of technology transfer to small businesses by government-sponsored innovation centres, Technology Analysis & Strategic Management, 4: 149-167.

OECD (1984). Committee for scientific and technological policy, science, technology and competitiveness, Analytical report of the Ad Hoc Group, Paris, OECD/STP (84) 26.

OECD, (1992). Technology and the Economy: The Key Relationships, Paris, OECD.

Pettigrew, A.M. (1985). The awakening giant: Continuity and Change in ICI, Basil Blackwell, Oxford.

Pettigrew, A.M. (1987). Introduction: Researching strategic change. I A.M. Pettigrew (red.) 1-13, The Management of strategic change, Basil Blackwell, Oxford.

Porter, M.E. (1985). Competitive advantage: Creating and sustaining superior performance, Free Press, New York.

Porter, M.E. (1990). The Competitive Advantage of Nations, MacMillan, London.

Prahlad, C.K. & Hamel, G. (1990). The Core Competence of the Corporation. Harvard Business Review, May-June.

Quinn, J.B. (1992). Intelligent Enterprise, Free Press, New York.

Reed, R. & R. De Fillippi (1990). Causal ambiguity, barriers to imitation, and sustainable competitive advantage, Academy of Management Review, 15: 88-102.

Rockart,F.R. & Short,J.E. (1988). Information Technology and the New Organization. Towards more Effective Management of Interdependence, M.I.T. W.P.1988-058.

Rogers, E.M. (1983), Diffusion of Innovations, New York, Free Press.

Rogers, E.M., & F.F. Shoemaker (1971). "Communication of innovations", Free Press, New York.

Rosenberg, N. (1982). Inside the Black Box: Technology and Economics, Cambridge University Press, Cambridge.

Rothwell, R. (1977). the characteristics of successful innovators and technically progressive firms (with some comments on innovation research), R&D Management, vol.7, no.3, 191-206.

Rothwell, R. (1991), "External Networking and Innovation in Small and Medium-Sized Manufacturing Firms in Europe", Technovation, 2: 93-112.

Rothwell, R. (1992). Successful industrial innovation: critical factors for the 1990´s, R&D Management, 22: 221-237.

Schumpeter, J. (1934). The theory of economic development, Harvard University Press,   Cambridge: Mass.

Schumpeter, J.A. (1942). Capitalism, Socialism and Democracy, Unwin, London (1987).

Scott Morton, M. S.(1991). The Corporation of the 1990s: Information Technology and Organizaional Transformation, Oxford University Press, New York.

Scott, M.F. (1989). A new View of Economic Growth, Clarendon Press, Oxford.

Scott, S.G. & R.A. Bruce (1994). Determinants of innovative behavior: A path model of   individual innovation in the workplace, Academy of Management Journal, 37: 580-607.

Senge, P.M. (1991). The Fifth Dicipline" , MIT Press.

Shepsle, K. & Weingast, B.(1987) "Why are Congressional Commitees Powerful?", American Political Science Review. 81: 935-945.

Slappendel, C. (1996). Perspectives on innovation in organizations, Organization Studies, 17,1: 107-129.

Smith, K. & T. Vidvei (1992). Innovation activity and innovation outputs in Norwegian   industry, Notat 3, NTNF-programmet: Fremtidsrettet teknologipolitikk.

Smith, K. (1994). New direction in research and technology policy: Identifying the key issues, STEP rapport, nr. 1, Oslo.

Soete, L. & A. Arundel (eds.). (1993). An integrated approach to European innovation and technology diffusion policy, Publication no. EKR 15090 EN of the Commission of the European Communities, Brussel.

Teece, D.J. (1986). Profiting from technological innovation: Implication for integration, collaboration, licensing and public policy. I D.J. Teece (red.) The competitive Challenge: Strategies for industrial innovation and Renewal, Ballinger, Cambridge, MA.

Teece, D.J. (1988). The nature and the structure of firms. I G. Dosi, C.Freeman, R.Nelson, G. Silverberg & L. Soete (red.). Technical Change and Economic Theory, Pinter, London.

Teece, D.J. (1989). Inter-organizational Requirements of the innovation process, Managerial and Decision Economics, Special Issue, 35-42.

Tusman, M. & D. Nadler (1986). Organizing for Innovation, California Management Review, vol. 28, 3: 74-92.

Utterback, J.M. (1982). Innovation in industry and the diffusion of technology. I M.L. Tushman & W.C. Moore (red.). 24-41, Readings in the management of innovation, Pitman, Boston.

Van de Ven, A. (1986). Central problems in the management of innovation, Management Science, vol. 32, 5: 590-607.

Van de Ven, A.A. & E.M. Rogers (1988). Innovations and organizations: Critical perspectives, Communication Research, 15: 623-651).

Van de Ven, A.A. & M.S. Poole (1988). Paradoxical requirements for a theory of organizational change. I R.E. Quinn & K.S. Cameron (red.). 19-63. Paradoxes and transformation: Toward a theory of change in organization and management, Ballinger, Cambridge:MA.

Van de Ven, A.A., H.L. Angle & M.S. Poole (red.). (1989). Research on the management of innovation: The Minesota studies, Harper & Row, New York.

Verspagen, B. (1992). Endogenous innovation in neo-classical growth models: A survey, Journal of Macro-Economics, vol. 14, no. 4: 631-662.

Von Hippel, E. (1986). Lead-users: A source of new Product Concepts, Management Science, Vpl. 32, no. 7: 791-805.

Von Hippel, E. (1988). The Sources of innovation, Oxford University Press, Oxford.

Von Hippel, E. (1989). Sources of Innovation, Oxford, London.

Walton, R.E. (1987). Innovation to compete, Jossey-Bass, San-Francisco.

Winter, S.G. (1987). Natural Selection and Evolution. I J. Eatwell, M. Milgate & P. Newman (red.). Vol.3: 614-617. The New Palgrave: A Dictionary of Economics, 4 vols, Macmillan, London.

World Bank, (1991). World Development Report, Oxford University Press, New York.

Womack, J. D. Jones & D. Roos (1990). The Machine that changed the world, Macmillian, New York.

Zaltman, G.R. (1973). Innovation and Organizations, John Wiley, New

York.

Ziman, J. (1991). A neural net model of innovation, Science & Public Policy, 18: 65-75.

Zirger, B.J. & M. Maidique (1990). A model of new product development: An empirical test, Management Science, 36: 867-883.

You, J.L. & F. Wilkinson (1994). Competition and Co-operation: Toward understanding industrial districs, Review of Political Economy, 6,3: 259-278.

CHAPTER 3 INNOVATION AND PERCOLATION

INTRODUCTION

Companies of today are facing an exponential advancements in technology, a frequent shifting in the nature of customer demand, and growing global competition, leading to increased turbulence and complexity in the business environment. D'Aveni (1994) categorizes the situation in its extreme form as hyper-competition. To meet these challenges, both the popular and the academic press are advising companies to focus their attention toward innovation in order to create and sustain competitive advantages (Porter, 2002). Porter (1990:780) says:"The process of innovation cannot be separated from a firms strategic and competitive context". Jacobson (1992) argues that it is the continuous changes in the state of knowledge that produce new disequilibrium situations and, therefore, new profit opportunities. Hence, we have seen an increased attention

toward innovation as the principal source of economic rent (Nelson and Winter, 1982; Nonaka and Takeuchi, 1995; Leonard-Barton, 1995; Grant, 1995, 1996; Spender and Grant, 1996; Baden-Fuller and Pitt, 1996, Davenport and Prusar, 1998).

Jacobsen (1992) argues that even though some profit opportunities are uncovered by pure chance, certain firms have more information than others, and that the existence of true profit depends on the possession of superior information. We argue, however, that the possession of superior information only represents a potential for true profits. MacPherson, (1997) found elaborate patterns of external knowledge acquisition to be prevalent among innovative firms that derived a substantial proportion of their current sales from new or significantly improved products. Conway (1995) findings suggest that sources external to the innovating organization account for between 34% and 65% of the inputs important to the development of a successful innovation. Hence, by systematizing and structuring information for the purpose of enhancing innovations, we argue that in developing knowledge appropriate for that purpose, it becomes important to acquire external knowledge.

Unfortunately for many companies, their innovations are often imitated, creating a dynamic competitive process. But, as the competitive process eliminates an opportunity, changes in the stream of knowledge produce other opportunities, which picture Shumpeter's (1909) vision of competition as a process of creative destruction, rather than as a static equilibrium condition.

Spender & Grant (1996) argue that the issue of imitability is central to the analysis of competitive advantage and its sustainability. Schendel (1996) argued that knowledge may be the key sources of rent, and that both the process by which knowledge is created and utilized in organizations may be the key inimitable resources managers need to appreciate, if not understand, if they would create sustainable rents.

We define knowledge as systematizing and structuring information for a specific purpose, which also pictures Libeskind´s (1996:94) definition of knowledge as "information whose validity has been established through tests of proof". Hence, a presupposition for creating knowledge is information, which underlines that information becomes the building block for knowledge, and that information processes of firms become paramount. We define information as: the difference in a message conducive to the perception of a difference relative to previous knowledge, or with Bateson: (1972:272) "the difference which make the difference".

Companies operating in hyper-competitive environments are heavily dependent upon external information in order to increase their innovative capacity, a prerequisite for creating and sustaining competitive advantages in such environments. This is consistent with a number of authors (e.g. Dodgeson, 1993; Freeman 1995), who argue that successful innovations presuppose an external orientation on the part of the companies, which in turn is dependent on external information scanning (Porter, 1990). Austere and Choo (1992, 1994) and Choo (1994) argue that external information scanning is the acquisition and use of information about events and trends in an external environment relative to organizations.

The essence of our argument is that the turbulence and complexity in the business environment is growing along with the need for external information in creating innovation (Huber, 1984; Grant, 1996a: 45), as innovation is seen as the primary strategic resource for companies in the knowledge economy (Drucker, 1993, Spender, 1996, Porter, 2002). Consequently, the underlying information processes in which external information is gathered and put into use are crucial for companies in their development of new knowledge, and ultimately their capacity to innovate and limit imitation. Hence, the research question in this chapter is: How can systemic knowledge processes create innovation and promote competitive advantages?

Fig. 1 Innovation and sustainable competitive advantages

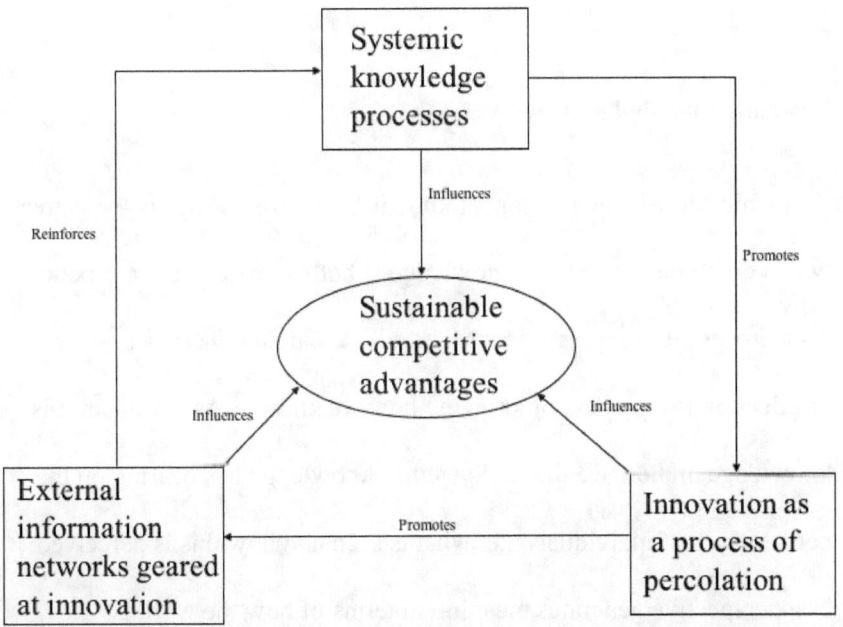

The chapter is organized as follows: First we discuss systemic knowledge processes. Then we discuss innovation as a process of percolation. The third stage is a discussion of external information networks geared at innovation. In each sections we summarize by showing which social mechanisms generates processes promoting sustainable competitive advantages.

Finally we will integrate the chapter by discussing sources of sustainable competitive advantages. In the conclusion a revisited model is designed building upon the discussion in the chapter which answer the research question.

Systemic knowledge processes

Systemic-knowledge is a sort of knowing how we know, i.e. the patterns which combine. Systemic- knowledge is both a process and a product. As a process it is expressed by Maturana & Varela (1987:24): "Reflection is a process of knowing how we know". As a product it is knowledge on how we think. Systemic-knowledge has bearing on the perspectives of individuals, i.e. what is seen and how this is perceived. The perspective generates meaning in terms of how the work is perceived and interpreted, in addition to adding input as to what a person is looking for in a job context. Systemic-knowledge is thus a form of split interpretation competence among the persons sharing the perspective. In this way systemic-knowledge directly influences these persons as to what type of explicit knowledge is relevant and meaningful for the company. The more uniform this perspective is among the most important actors of the company, the more influential this perspective will be as to what knowledge type (e.g. explicit versus tacit) is critical to the competitive position of the company. The persons in the company who have various degree of systemic-knowledge or different basis perspectives, will be able to view the same phenomenon, but interpret it differently, giving it various meanings relative to the opportunities and challenges of the company.

Knowledge integration is the essence of "organizational capabilities" (Grant, 1996: 377) and "The wider the span of knowledge being integrated the more complex are the problems of creating and managing organizational capability". It is the integration of the knowledge types of individuals (task-related, experience-based and functional knowledge) into systemic knowledge which expresses a company's organizational "capability". This has also been expressed by Tsuokas (1966:22) who focuses on "those lower down" in the hierarchy " finding more and more ways of getting connected and interrelating the knowledge each one has". The knowledge base of the company is in other words just the starting point on their road to "capability". It is only when the knowledge base is integrated to transform input into output for the purpose of increasing values that the company's capability of execution is increased. Hence, in a situation were knowledge is seen as the most important strategic factor in creating innovation and sustainable competitive advantages, and where the main separating line in knowledge categorization is drawn between the tacit and explicit parts of the knowledge base, it is knowledge integration, more so than knowledge development, which becomes the focal point.

Parts of literature points to rules and routines as a way of integrating the tacit part of knowledge (Demsetz, 1991: 172). But the main point of tacit knowledge is that:" we can know more than we can tell". (Polanyi, 1983: 4), and rules and routines can not alone manage to capture this knowledge. Hence, when companies try to emphasize this type of knowledge by means of rules and routines, one will discover that a considerable part of this type of knowledge cannot be captured, and companies will experience "substantial knowledge loss" (Grant, 1996: 379). On the other hand information routines, communication routines and interactive learning routines embody the propensity for capturing part of the tacit knowledge (Pentland and Rueter, 1994).

It is more the pattern of interactions in organizations based on problem proximity, context understanding and personal experiences which could carry the hope of uncovering tacit knowledge, as shown by Nonaka and Tackeuchi (1995).

The possibilities of combining different types of knowledge, is by Kogut and Zander (1992) referred to as "combinative capabilities", and it may appear that it is exactly through various types of combinations that new knowledge grows, as pointed out by Grant (1996).

One important point in focusing on knowledge integration is that knowledge is possessed by individuals, and they can easily transfer their services to competing companies. However, if systems of a systemic nature are developed in companies, i.e. that the knowledge of individuals is put together in integrated coherent systems, ensuring that each individual must be part of a larger system to be able to exploit his personal knowledge base, the transition to other companies will be difficult, and imitation will too. The prerequisite for effective integration of individual knowledge is the existence of effective information, communication and learning systems in the company. The absence of these systems swill split up the company knowledge base among atomized actors who also have more difficulty in exploiting the knowledge of others in the company. This will also reduce the capacity for interpretation and transmission of information from the environment, which could be of crucial importance to the ability to create and maintain sustainable competitive advantages.

It seems likely that knowledge which is publicly accessible cannot be exploited by all companies with the same end result. The application and results of knowledge will depend on the existing knowledge base of the company. In this way we have made a statement that open exchange of information does not mean that recipients of this information can use it in the same manner. Open and accessible information will lead to differences in terms of application and results among the various companies making use of it. The open exchange of information is thus advantageous for all participants who both contribute and share knowledge. This could explain why companies to a major extent share information on various information meeting grounds. It is a win-win situation for all parties involved. It is the application of the common knowledge base linked to the company-specific knowledge base which seems to create the innovative novelty. This complies with the main arguments of the resource-based theory (Lado et. al., 1992; Dierikx and Cool, 1989; Barney, 1986). We also find support for this line of arguments with Freeman and Soete (1990) in addition to Romer (1986). This indicates that innovation can not be seen as a purely internal activity in the innovative company, but as a larger social process, where external information processes play an important part, and where the environment in which the company operate becomes crucial for the innovative power of the individual company. This brings us to the cluster theory and innovation.

Cluster as a competitive factor has a long-standing historical basis. It was, however, only with increased knowledge intensity both in input, process, and output, in addition to globalisation of the economy, that both the depth and scope of cluster grow into a decisive factor for competitive strategies of companies. "Cluster represents a new and complementary way of understanding an economy, organising economic development, and setting public policy" (Porter, 1998: 266). The competitive situation for the individual enterprise is usually regarded from the perspective of what materialises on the inside of the system's boundaries. This has also been the case with a nation's competitive situation. For the individual enterprise a consequence of cluster thinking is that instrategy thinking the larger system of which one is part serves as the starting poin: The health of the cluster is important to the health of the company" (Porter, 1998: 198). The role of the authorities in this context will be to remove obstacles and promote cluster development, since cluster furthers export and attracts foreign capital.

There are three factors that can explain the genesis and development of cluster (Porter, 1998: 25).

1. The degree of local competition
2. The conditions for the establishment of new enterprises
3. The degree of structural links in the geographical field

When in turn a critical mass of enterprises is established in the region, the cluster will develop self-enforcing social mechanisms, perpetuating further development.

The theoretical basis for the cluster theory is found with Alfred Marshall (1890). An increasing interest in cluster theory appears in the 1990s with, among others, Krugman (1995) and Porter (1990; 1998). Porter (1998:266) says that cluster is a new way of understanding economic organisations in developed economies subject to global competition. Porter (1990) has in his theory for the competitive position of nations put cluster in a very prominent role. Porter (1998: 197 – 198) defines cluster in the following way: "Clusters are geographic concentration of interconnected companies, specialized suppliers, service providers, firms in related industries, and associated institutions (e.g. universities, standards agencies, and trade association) in particular fields that compete but also cooperate". A further link between cluster theory and systemic thinking has been made by Porter (1998: 213), briefly explaining the essence of cluster: a system of connected firms and institution whose value as a whole is greater than the sum of its parts". This makes the construct emergence central for cluster theory as much as for systemic thinking.

In the global economy there are three main factors having been pointed out by Porter (1998: 209) regarding businesses capable of competing: the degree of development in the cluster in whichh the businesses operate, productivity and the innovative potential of the businesses. Productivity and innovative potential are, in fact, stimulated by their being established in a well-developed cluster. The presence of well-educated persons, effective public institutions and the absence of bureaucratic hindrances give indications as to the degree of development on the part of a cluster.

To think in terms of cluster will from a competitive point of view be important both for the individual business and the formation of the economic policy carried out by the authorities. A positive economic effect of clusters is, among other things, that they promote the establishment of new businesses stimulated by innovations made in the cluster. Another effect of cluster is the reduction of transaction costs, among other things because the input factors are cheaper and the fact that time lags are reduced.

The more developed the cluster, the more businesses are represented. This is evident from Porter's diamond (1990) and is underlined by Porter (2002). The competitive position of the individual company is to a greater extent determined by the degree of development on the part of the cluster, and to a lesser extent on the size of the individual business or trade in the cluster (Porter, 1998:215). I will also be easier to attract specialised employees form other places in the region when developed cluster exist (Rauch, 1993).

In the same way as the costs of input factors are reduced in clusters, similarly costs relative to information processes are reduced. For analytical reasons we choose to denote the former as transaction costs and the latter as transformation costs. Transformation costs are reduced due to the fact that it becomes easier to understand the needs linked to placing orders, being a customer, user, etc, in addition to clusters being strongly internally linked (Saxenian, 1994).

A well-developed cluster can also have well-developed complementary offers, not only for the individual final buyer, but also for local requesters of services in the cluster. This is organised through a well-developed system of sub-suppliers. Businesses in clusters quickly manage to grasp new trends and changes in the needs of customers. The reason for this is density, the strength of structural links in the cluster, the access to information and the spill-over effects operating in cluster.

If we compare clusters in more developed economies to clusters in less developed economies, the main difference to be noticed is that companies in clusters in developed economies are exposed to a much fiercer international competition than companies in less developed economies (see Porter, 1998: 233). During the exposure to global competition, productivity and the degree of innovation are furthered. Low-cost strategies will only to a limited extent be appropriate in developed economies, since developed economies will never be able to compete with the cost structure of less developed economies. Developed economies compete on the basis of innovative clusters with a high degree of productivity (see Porter, 2002: XX). If the purpose is to develop material prosperity, the challenge will be to further productivity and innovative ability (see porter, 1998: 234). There appears to be a direct link between the degree of development in a cluster and the per capita income (opcit). The two most central factors capable of distorting the position of clusters, are change in technology and competition. They can be changed irrespectively of each other and in interaction with each other (Porter, 1998: 236).

One interesting point in cluster thinking is that it may be fruitful to focus on the boundaries between two or more clusters. In this boundary area there might be potential for the development of unique products or service opportunities. These may then be developed into new specialised products.

One effect of cluster development might be businesses re-establishing themselves in the region and national and international investments being attracted. This furthermore re-enforces the degree of development in the cluster. Special competence is attracted, causing the cluster to be further reinforced. In this way structural links in the cluster are developed.

Basically there are four factors of critical importance to the possible success of a cluster. These are the four factors in Porters diamond (1990): Iput factors, context factors, demand factors and complementary factors. Authorities play a major part in the development of institutions, which, among other things, should ensure that the four main factors are instrumental in promoting clusters in a region.

If productivity and the degree of innovation for some reason are hindered, this will lead to a reduction in the competitive ability of the cluster. The cluster will then initiate the process leading to its own disintegration (Porter, 2002). External conditions capable of threatening the development of a cluster are, among other things, technological, economic and political changes. Technological and economic changes can lead to changes in demand and thus rapidly alter the competitive environment of the cluster. Political changes can lead to an altered business climate, influencing the competitive environment negatively.

Political stability helps sustain expectations over a period of time, which will further the development of trust between the various actors in the economic field.

While the paradigm of industrial policy was/is oriented toward scale and scope, then the cluster paradigm is oriented towards productivity and innovation (see Porter, 1998:249)

It is then not only internal knowledge development and company-internal learning systems which create knowledge and innovation. Even more important is the type of knowledge developed in other companies and institutions. An implication of this is that investments in internal R&D environments, internal knowledge development and internal organizational learning systems may be important, but even more important is the link between these activities and information and communication processes focusing on company-external processes. The line of argument points out that R&D activities, if located in the individual companies or in specific knowledge situations, constitute only a minor part of the "virtual" knowledge or R&D processes. The virtual knowledge processes consist of external information and communication processes, the existing knowledge base of the company, the receptiveness for information in companies, plus the connection structure of companies relative to other companies and institutions in the environment. Consequently, the focus of our knowledge investments must be transferred from the classical R&D and knowledge institutions, to the links between various systems generating knowledge, i.e. a systemic knowledge point of view. This is also supported by Cohen and Leventhal (1989).

That information and communication processes are important for organizational learning processes has, been argued for by Powell (1990), Zucker (1991) and Grant (1996). The main emphasis in literature related to organizational knowledge and learning: "is on the acquisition of information by organization" (Grant, 1996: 376). If it turns out that information, communication, and learning processes are crucial for the development and integration of knowledge, these processes will constitute necessary conditions for innovation and subsequently the sustainable competitive advantages of the company, as the positive relationship between knowledge an innovation and between innovation and sustainable competitive advantages is well established in the literature. It will thus be information processes, communication processes and organizational learning processes which should be the focal entities to ensure the survival of the company and the creation of sustainable competitive advantages. It is these processes which enable organizations to develop tacit and explicit knowledge. The resource-based view and the knowledge theory (Grant, 1995; 1996; 1996a) argue that tacit knowledge is paramount in creating and sustaining competitive advantages. However, this does not, imply that the explicit knowledge should be toned down, but rather that explicit knowledge is seen as a necessary precondition, while tacit knowledge is seen as a sufficient precondition, for sustainable competitive advantages.

The model which can be generated from the discussion in this section is shown in fig. 2. In the model we argue that routines for information-communication and organizational learning systems, problem proximity, context understanding, personal experience, system dependency are social mechanisms which trigger integration processes and in turn promotes sustainable competitive advantages.

Fig. 2 Systemic knowledge

Model element	Social mechanisms	Processes	Phenomenon
Systemic knowledge	Routines for information,- communication and organizational learning systems Problem proximity, context-understanding, personal experience Systemdependency	Integration-processes	Sustainable competitive advantages

Innovation as a process of percolation

Percolation processes have been studied in physics as the outcome of two classes of forces termed as connectivity and receptivity. Antonelli (1996) used the term in studying information networks and argued that connectivity can be used as a measure of the number of connections in place among the agents in the network, and also that receptivity can be used as a measure of the capacity of each agent to absorb the information received. We argue that external meeting places and the use of electronic media may be regarded as a firm connectivity, while sensitivity to change may be seen as the firms receptivity. We find some support for this line of argument in Premkumar and Ramamurthy (1995), who, when evaluating the differences between proactive and reactive firms, concluded that proactive firms were found to have a greater extent of adaptation, more external connectivity and a better integration of electronic data interchange (EDI) information.

Gupta and Wilemon (1996) found that successful R&D managers were categorized as being sensitive to changes in the business environment, maintaining a spirit of inquiry. Song et al. (1997) further argue that sensitivity to customer wants and needs are paramount for successful innovations. This might also be viewed in light of a firm's proactiveness. Ashford and Black (1996) argue that information and feedback seeking are seen as proactive activities. Also, Premkumar and Ramamurthy (1995) argue that proactive firms are found to have a greater extent of adoption and more external connectivity. Lumpkin and Dess (1996:146) argue that "....a proactive firm is a leader rather than a follower, because it has the will and the foresight to seize new opportunities". They make a distinction between competitive aggressiveness and proactiveness, where proactiveness has to do with meeting demand, whereas competitive aggressiveness is about competing for demand. Hence, we argue that sensitivity to change first has a direct effect on the firms innovativeness, and second, that it is also a prerequisite for seeking the kind of information that will enable the firm to meet the future demand of customers through external meeting places, and by using electronic media.

Information richness theory (Daft and Lengel, 1986) argues that communication media vary in their capacity to process rich information. In order of decreasing richness, the media classification are (1) face-to-face, (2) telephone, (3) personal documents such as letters and memos, (4) impersonal written documents, and (5) numeric documents. Lee (1994:143) argued that: "In the view of information richness theory, electronic mail filters out important cues such as body language and tone of voice and, unlike face-to-face meetings, is not conducive to immediate feedback". Markus (1994) did, however, argue that because e-mail can offer faster communication than chapter-based documents, most analysts have rated it as falling somewhere between the telephone and non-electronic written communications in richness. Huber (1990) further argues that the use of information technology leads to a quicker retrieval of information. Kessler and Chakrabarti (1996) argued, after an extensive literature review, that there is a growing recognition of speed as an important factor in the development of successful innovations. In order for firms to be able to initiate innovations within a turbulent and complex environment, they need fast access to information. Hence, the positive relation between using electronic media as information channels and innovation might be due to the increasingly ready access to information, which in turn will enhance innovations.

Although the use of electronic media is important for innovation, it is limited to the transfer of knowledge which is easily communicated to others as information. Howels (1996) argues that tacit knowledge has become recognized as playing a key role in economic competitiveness. Hence, tacit knowledge is probably the part of the knowledge base which, in the knowledge society, will constitute the difference generating sustainable competitive advantages. We argue that external meeting places constitute an arena where tacit knowledge can be converted to explicit knowledge. This is also underlined by Nonaka and Takeuchi (1995), referring to the psychological closeness of the interaction between individuals at such meeting places, and the richness of information media.

External information scanning can be seen in a network perspective, where information is obtained and forwarded in distinct knowledge networks, such as among firms, and at conferences. This is a form of breath of the knowledge base for the firms which are found to increase the sustainability of competitive advantages (Reed and DeFillipi, 1990; Leonard-Barton, 1995). This also renders possibilities for the integration of different knowledge streams which in some studies are linked to higher performance (Henderson & Cockburn, 1994; Pisano, 1994). Powell (1990) argues that it is through social networks that companies most effectively can acquire information. It is particularly the confidence in information inherent in this type of networks which Powell argues in favor of. Companies electing to acquire information from this type of external meeting places will have a major learning potential, according to Powell, since the quality of information and the relevance will be greater than would be the case with information acquired through other media. Daft and Lengel (1986:560) also argue that: "In a sense, richness pertains to the learning capacity of communication" These meeting places for information sharing provide organizations with information which have a positive effect on their performance, according to Zucker (1991: 164) and Appleyard (1996: 151), since, according to Grant (1996), it is acquired in a context characterized by "open-ended learning". Another motivation for being active in this kind of meeting places, is the potential for increased organizational flexibility, with ready access to "private" information not normally available elsewhere (Hick, 1995), often dealing with circumstantial factors with a low degree of predictability. " Firms that share knowledge often receive knowledge in the process" (Appleyard, 1996: 151). This is further underlined in an empirical study of the difference between the Silicon Valley success story and the relative stagnation on Route 128 (Saxenian, 1994). The organization can then, based on this private information, adjust more quickly to meet these changes (D'Aveni, 1994; Volberda, 1996). Both the uncertainty and ambiguity of information can be reduced through active participation at these information grounds (Appleyard, 1996), as both the quality of information and the mutual trust between people who meet here will contribute to the realization of this (Zucker, 1991). An important purpose of external meeting places will be to take advantage of knowledge related to e.g. innovative technology having been developed externally. It is this very link between company-specific knowledge and knowledge developed in e.g. other companies, which through external meeting places as described here, could generate the type of knowledge needed to trigger innovations, and thereby competitive advantages not easily imitated by other (Lippman and Rumelt, 1982).

The model which can be generated from the discussion in this section is shown in fig. 3. In the model we argue that external meeting places, use of electronic media and sensitivity to change are social mechanisms which trigger connectivity and receptivity and in turn promotes sustainable competitive advantages.

Fig. 3 Innovation as a process of percolation

Model element	Social mechanisms	Processes	Phenomenon
Percolation	External meeting places, use of electronic media	Connectivity	Sustainable competitive advantages
	Sensitivity to change	Receptivity	

3. External information networks geared at innovation

Nonaka and Takeuchi (1995) argue that a prerequisite for developing and integrating knowledge is the existence of information processes, communication processes and learning processes within firms. Information and communication processes as underlying mechanisms for knowledge integration is also underlined by Van de Ven et al. (1986). We further argue that the acquisition of external information through external information scanning is the building block for the development, integration and application of the knowledge needed to enhance innovations. Our main focus is therefore on information processes related to the acquisition of external information, as we argue that in order for the acquisition, development, integration and application of knowledge to be effective in organizations, understanding the process by which appropriate external information is acquired becomes paramount. The essence of our argument is that an important prerequisite for developing new knowledge involves information processes where information contacts, information channels and information behavior are essential.

Sweeney (1996) argues that we are always in the process of acquiring new information. Some is used immediately, some is passed on as being of perceived use to others, and some is retained in the memory to be recalled by some future event. Auster and Choo (1994) found in a study of the Canadian publishing and telecommunication industries that in the majority of cases, the chief executives used environmental information in the entrepreneur's decisional role, initiating new products, projects or policies. The literature presents a number of information contacts believed to influence the propensity on the part of firms to innovate. The importance of the relationship between information from customers and innovation has received increased attention from the late 1960's. Myers and Marquis' (1969) study of more than 500 innovative companies confirmed the importance of information from customers and close customer relations as crucial for the development of innovations. This is also consistent with the findings of Mowery and Rosenberg (1982), and is strongly emphasized by Andersen (1994:57), who points out that: "-- firms with well-established information channels to sophisticated customers have a comparative advantage in the creation of innovations". Also, Karakaya and Kobu (1994) found that using customers as the sources of new product ideas ranks number one in terms of importance for businesses.

Lundvall (1988) strongly emphasize the user-producer connectivity, and argues that innovation is enhanced through a process of learning by interacting. Customers as an important source of innovations has also been pointed out by Von Hippel (1986), Deshpande et al. (1993), the European Commission's Green Chapter on Innovation (1995) and Craig (1995). Moenaret and Caeldries (1996) argued that an effective R&D organization needs information from a complex web of sources, including suppliers and customers. Close interactions with suppliers to enhance innovativeness is also pointed out by Lundvall (1988) and Håkansson (1989). Others have pointed out the importance of information from competitors and distributors as sources of innovative success, both through formal and informal contacts (e.g. Von Hippel, 1987, 1988; Slaughter, 1993; OECD, 1988; Imai, 1989; Karakaya and Kobu 1994). An important part of the company's environment is constituted by the public sector, both as a regulatory body, and through various public investments and direct support for companies. It would therefore be of interest to know whether having information contacts in these environments will have an effect on firms innovativeness.

Choo (1994) argues that internal and personal sources of information are more important than external impersonal sources, as they are perceived to be more reliable and to provide more relevant information. Link and Rees (1990) found that large corporations benefit more from their own R&D activities in comparison with small firms, while small firms tend to benefit more from spillovers from research undertaken in research laboratories. Audretsch and Vivarelli (1996) indicated that (:256) "not only do such R&D spillovers exist but that they are stronger for small firms than their larger counterparts", indicating that small firms are able to innovate by exploiting knowledge created outside the firm.

Information is facilitated through information channels. Auster and Choo (1994) found personal sources to be important for information on customers and competitors, whereas printed or formal sources were important for information on technological and regulatory matters. Auster and Choo (1992) found newschapters and periodicals to be important media for the acquisition of information. Others have found that managers in innovative firms read more scientific literature and also exploit more trade chapters and professional literature (Tushman, 1977; Tushman and Scanlan, 1981; Allen, 1978).

Zaremba (1996) argues that despite the technological sophistication of e-mail, questions remain regarding the value of the innovation for organizations. However, Lee (1994) found that managers who receive e-mail are not passive recipients of data, but active producers of meaning. Also, Kruger and Struzzerio (1997) found, in studying the use of e-mail among school psychologists, that the majority of messages contributed to the school psychologists becoming more knowledgeable about consultation and knowing what support to offer the other school psychologists. They also perceived their computer-mediated group to be highly cohesive.

Increased turbulence, complexity, uncertainty and dependency of knowledge leads to increased acquisition of external information (Daft et al., 1988). Communication media vary in their capacity to process rich information. This has caused managers operating in such an environment to prefer media that is rich on information (Kurke and Alerich, 1993), e.g. verbal and face-to-face meetings. Sweeney (1996) argues that the reason why we prefer face-to-face communication is that it has a richness unattainable in any other mode of communication. We argue that external information provided on external meeting places provides the means by which tacit knowledge (Polanyi, 1966) can be converted to explicit knowledge. This is also underlined by Nonaka and Takeuchi

(1995). Daft and Lengel (1986:560) argue that: "Face-to-face is the richest medium because it provides immediate feedback so that interpretation can be checked. Face to face also provides multiple cues via body language and tone of voice, and message content is expressed in natural language". Sweeney (1996:8) argues that: "Such is the richness of face-to-face contact that were there is a frequent use of personal contact, there is a high level of creativity. Solutions to problems are found more efficiently, they are more creative, and innovative ideas are more frequently generated".

Furthermore, empirical findings indicate that innovative individuals are members of numerous professional bodies, and maintain a more extensive external network than non-innovative individuals (Tushman, 1977; Tushman og Scanlan, 1981; Allen, 1978). These findings indicate that innovators have a strong external network. It is also fair to assume that time spent by management on maintaining external contacts pays in terms of improving the company's ability to reach their goals, as pointed out by Kefalas and Schodebek (1973). One potentially important network is formed by professional associations, as it creates informal networks of members from different organizations. Newell and Swan (1995) found that professional association networks are important for innovation.

The model which can be generated from the discussion in this section is shown in fig. 4. In the model we argue that information contacts, information channels and information behavior are social mechanisms which trigger external information scanning and in turn promotes sustainable competitive advantages.

Fig. 4 External information networks geared at innovation

Model element	Social mechanisms	Processes	Phenomenon
Networking	Information contacts Information channels Information behavior	External information scanning	Sustainable competitive advantages

Conclusion

In explaining sustainable competitive advantages, the literature presents two major paradigms, the industrial organization (IO) theory, which is built on neoclassical micro-economic theory, and the resource-based view. According to neoclassical micro-economic theory, profit-maximizing firms in competitive environments earn zero economic profit. They earn a return just sufficient to maintain capital investments (Jacobsen, 1992). Hence, firms need to exercise monopoly power in order to make supernormal profits. To achieve this, the IO-theory focuses externally on the industry and product markets, and is based on the assumption that sustainable competitive advantages are possible by limiting competitive forces through creating entry barriers at the industry level (exercising monopoly power). Or with Porter, (1980:4) who argues that: "the strategic objective of the firm is to position itself in an industry where it can defend itself against competitive forces". This approach is concentrating on market conditions which are in equilibrium, advocating a static notion of the nature of competition. However, today most companies face a turbulent an complex business environment, often in turmoil, heading for an unpredictable and unstable future. Within this picture, the IO approach has been criticized for a lack of attention to such dynamic environments (e.g. Nelson and Winter, 1982). Solow (1997: 33-34) points out that steady state situations (equilibrium) are convenient but they are less and less relevant in a turbulent globalized, hypercompetitive environment. Hence, as argued by Grant (1996: 375): "If market structure is in a state of flux, and if monopoly rents quickly succumb to new sources of competition, approaches to strategy based upon product markets and positioning within them are unlikely to yield profit advantages that are more than temporary".

The resource-based view, conceptually rooted in Penrose's (1959) theory of the firm, has an underlying theoretical approach whereby the firms are seen as a unique bundle of tangible and intangible sources and not through their activities in the product market. The notion of invisible assets (Itami and Roehl, 1987) and the core competence of an organization (Prahalad and Hamel, 1990) are important elements. Hence, this view argues that competitive effectiveness is a function of the firms' ability to create idiosyncratic, relatively inimitable resource endowments, which then become strategic assets (Amit and Schoemaker, 1993).

As an extension of the resource-based view we have seen an increased focus on knowledge as being of vital importance to business (e.g., Quinn, 1992; Drucker, 1993). On the theoretical level we have seen the emergence of the knowledge-based theory (Grant, 1996, 1996a), and the theory of organizational knowledge creation (Nonaka et al. 1996). The underlying assumption of these approaches is that knowledge is the principal productive resource of the firm. The cornerstone of the epistemology related to these theoretical approaches is the distinction between tacit and explicit knowledge. Explicit knowledge is the part of the knowledge base which is easily communicated to others as information, while tacit knowledge, which is woven into a tradition of which the actors are a part (Nonaka, 1994), is the part of the knowledge base which is not easily communicated to others as information. The concept of tacit knowledge, introduced by Polanyi (1966) is related to observation, imitation and the use of knowledge, where the key is experience over a certain period of time in a specific context (Rolf, 1995), or with Nonaka et al. (1996:834) "tacit knowledge is personal, context-specific, and therefore hard to formalize and communicate". A number of researchers (Howells, 1996; Sveiby, 1997; Stewart, 1997) argue that tacit knowledge previously, for the most part, has been neglected by academics and managers. This is clearly expressed by Howells (1996: 91): "Just as technological innovation up until the 1960's was treated as an unexplained variance in economic growth and performance, so tacit knowledge as an element within technological innovation has, until recently, been seen in a similar way". This development has lately changed toward a stronger focus on tacit knowledge (Nonaka, 1994; Nonaka and Takeuchi, 1995, Grant, 1996) and is now recognized as playing a key role in firm growth and economic competitiveness. Within the literature, the resource-based view and the knowledge-based theory have captured the tacit dimension with an emphasis on invisible resources and the internal capabilities within firms (Kought and Zander, 1992; Amit and Shoemaker, 1993; Conner and Pralahad, 1996, Grant, 1996). The emphasis on tacit knowledge is a result of a growing globalization (Thurow, 1997) and hyper-competition (D´aveni, 1994), where the concept of success is resting on the ability of firms to limit imitation and enhance innovation. Hence, in order to succeed within such a business environment, firms need to capture both the explicit and tacit dimension of knowledge.

The model which can be generated from the discussion in the chapter is shown in fig. 5.

Fig. 5 How can systemic knowledge processes create innovation and promote competitive advantages?

Model element	Social mechanisms	Processes	Phenomenon
Systemic knowledge	Routines for information,- communication- and organizational learning systems Problem proximity, context- understanding, personal experience	Integration- processes	Sustainable competitive advantages
Percolation	Systemdependency Ekternal meeting places, use of electronic media Sensitivity to change	Connectivity Receptivity	
Networking	Information contacts Information channels Information behavior	External information scanning	

REFERENCES

Acs, Z.J. and Audretsch, D.B. (1990). *Innovation and Small Firms*. Cambridge: MIT Press.

Afifi, A.A. and C. Clark (1990). *Computer aided multivariate analysis (2nd edition)*. Van Nostrand Reinhold Company, NY.

Allen, T.J (1978). *Managing the flow of technology: Technology transfer and the dissemination of technological information within the research and development organization*. MIT Press, Cambridge, MASS

Amit, R. and. Schoemaker, P.J.H. (1993). "Strategic assets and organizational rent". *Strategic Management Journal*, **14**(99), pp. 33-46.

Andersen, E.S. (1994). *Evolutionary Economics: Post-Schumperterian Contributions*. Pinter, London.

Antonelli, C. (1996). "Localized knowledge percolation and information networks". *Journal of Evolutionary Economics*, **6**(3), Aug, pp. 281-295.

Appleyard, M.M. (1996). "How does knowledge flow? Interfirm patterns in the semiconductor industry". *Strategic Management Journal*, **17** (Special Issue), pp.137-154.

Ashford, S.J. and Black, J.S. (1996). "Proactivity during organizational entry: The role of desire for control". *Journal of Applied Psychology*. **81**(2), April, pp. 199-214.

Audretsch, D.B, and Vivarelli. M. (1996)."Firm Size and R&D spillovers: Evidence from Italy". *Small Business Economics*, **18**(3), pp. 249-258.

Auster, E. and Choo, C.W. (1992). "Environmental scanning- preliminary findings on a survey of CEO information seeking behavior in 2 Canadian industries". *Proceedings of the Asis Annual Meeting.* **29**, pp. 48-54.

Auster, E. and Choo, C.W. (1994). "How senior manager acquire and use information in environmental scanning". *Information Processing and Management*. **30**(5), Sept-Oct, pp.607-618.

Baden-Fuller, C., and Pitt, M. (1996). "The nature of innovating strategic management". In C. Baden-Fuller and Pitt, M. (eds.), *Strategic Innovation*, Routledge, London, pp. 3-42.

Barney, J.B. (1986). "Strategic factor markets: Expectations, luck, and business strategy". *Management Science*, **21**, pp. 489-506.

Barton, D.L. (1995). *Wellsprings of Knowledge: Building and Sustaining the Sources of Innovation*, Harvard Business School Press, Boston, MASS.

Bateson, G. (1972). *Steps to a ecology of mind*. Intex Books, London.

Biemans, W.G. (1989). *Developing Innovations Within Networks*, PhD Thesis, Eindhoven, the Netherlands.

Brown, S. L., and Eisenhardt (1995). "Product development: Past research, present findings, and future directions". *Academy of*

Management Review. **20**(2), pp. 343-378.

Bryman, A. and D. Cramer (1990). *Quantitative data analysis for social scientists.* Routledge, London.

Brynjolfsson, E (1993). "The productivity paradox of information technology", *Comm. ACM,* **35**, pp. 66-77.

Campbell, D. T., and Fiske, D. W. (1959). "Convergent and discriminant validation by the multitrait-multimethod matrix". *Psychological Bulletin,* **54**(2), pp. 81-105.

Chatterjee, S. and Price, B. (1977). *Regression analysis by example,* Wiley, NY.

Choo, C.W. (1994). "Perception and use of information-sources by chief executives in environmental scanning". *Library & Information Science Research.* **16**(1) Winter, pp.23-40.

Clark, K.B., and Fujimoto, T. (1991). *Product development performance,* Harvard Business School Press, Boston.

Cohen, L., and Holliday, M. (1982). *Statistics for Social Scientists,* Harper & Row, London

Cohen, W.M., and Levinthal, D.A. (1989). " Innovation and learning: The two faces of R&D". *Economic Journal,* **99**, pp. 569-596.

Cohen, W., and Levinthal, P. (1990). "Absorptive capacity: A new perspective on learning and innovation", *Administrative Science Quarterly,* **35**(1), pp. 128-152.

Conway, S. (1995). "Informal boundary-spanning communication in the innovation process- An empirical study". *Technology Analysis & Strategic Management.* **7**(3), pp.327-342.

Conner, K.R., and Prahalad, C.K. (1996). "A resource-based theory of the firm: Knowledge versus opportunism", *Organization Science,* **7**(5), pp. 477-501.

Cornish. S.L. (1997). "Product innovation and the spatial dynamics of market intelligence: Does proximity to markets matter?" *Economic*

Geography. **73**(2), April, pp.143-165.

Craig, T. (1996). "The Japanese Beer wars; Initiating and responding to hypercompetition in new product development", *Organizational Science*, **7**(3), pp. 302-321.

Daft, R.L. (1992). *Organization theory and design*, West St. Paul, MN.

Daft, R.L., and Lengel, R.H. (1986). "Organizational information requirement, media richness and structural design", *Management Science*, **32**(5), pp. 554-571.

Daft, R.L., Sormunen, J., and Parks, D. (1988). "Chief executive scanning, environmental characteristics, and company performance. An empirical study". *Strategic Management Journal*, **9**, pp. 123-139.

Damanpour, F. (1996). "Organizational complexity and innovation: Developing and testing multiple contingency models". *Management Science*, **42**(5), pp. 693-716.

Damanpour, F., and Evan, V.M. (1984)."Organizational innovation and performance. The problem of organizational lag", *Administrative Science Quarterly*, **29**, Sept., pp. 392-409.

D´Aveni, R (1994). *Hypercompetition: The dynamics of strategic maneuvering*, Basic Books, New York

Davenport, T.H. and Prusar, L. (1998). *Working knowledge: How organizations manage what they know*. Harvard Business School Press, Boston.

Davis, C.D., Hill G.E., and LaForge. T. (1985). "The Marketing/Small Enterprise Paradox, a Research Agenda". *International Small Business Journal* **3**(3), pp. 31-42.

Demsetz, H. (1991). "The theory of the firm revised", in O.E. Williamson and S.Winter (Eds), *The nature of the firm,* Mew York: Oxford University Press, pp. 198-178.

Deshpande, R., Farley, J.U., and Webster, F.E jr. (1993). "Corporate Culture, customer orientation and innovation in Japanese firms: A quadrate analysis". *Journal of Marketing*, **57**(1), pp. 23-37.

Dodgeson, E.M. (1993). *Technological collaberation in inustry, strategy, policy and internalisation in innovation,* Oxford University Press, London.

DosSantos, B.L., Peffers, K.G., and Mauer, D,C. (1993). "The impact of information technology investment announcements on the market value of the firm", *Information Systems Research*, **4**(1), pp. 1-23.

Drazin, R., and Schoonhoven, C. B. (1996). "Community, population, and organization effects on innovation: A multilevel perspective". *Academy of Management Journal*, **39**(5), pp. 1065-1083.

Drucker, P.F.(1993). *Post-capitalist Society*. Butterworth Heineman, New York.

European Commission. 1995. *Green chapter on innovation.* Brussels.

Feldman, M.P. (1994). "Knowledge Complementary and Innovation". *Small Business Economics*, **6**, pp.363-372.

Freeman, C. (1995). "The National System of Innovation in Historical Perspective". *Cambridge Journal of Economics,* **19**, pp. 5-24.

Freeman, C., and Soete, L. (1990). *New explorations in the economics of technological change*, Pinter, London.

Grant, R.M. (1995). *Contemporary strategy analysis: Concepts, Techniques, Applications*, Blackwell, Cambridge, MA.

Grant, R.M. (1996). "Prospering in dynamically-competitive environments: Organizational capability as knowledge integration", *Organizational Science,* **7**(4), pp. 375-387.

Grant, R.M. (1996a). "Toward a knowledge-based theory of the firm". *Strategic Management Journal,* **17** (Winter Special Issue), pp. 109-122.

Gupta, A.K., and Wilemon, D. (1996). "Changing patterns in industrial R&D management". *Journal of Product Innovation Management.* **13**(6), Nov., pp. 497-511.

Henderson, R. and Cockburn, I. (1994). "Managing innovation in the information age". *Harvard Business Review,* **72**(3), pp. 100-105.

Hicks, D. (1995). "Published chapters, tacit competencies and corporate management of the public/private character of knowledge". *Industrial and Corporate Change,* **4**(2). pp. 401-24.

Howells, J. (1996). "Tacit knowledge, innovation and technology transfer". *Technology Analysis & Strategic Management,* **8**(2), pp. 91-106.

Huber, G. (1984). "The nature and design of Post-industrial organizations". *Management Science,* **30**, pp. 928-951.

Huber, G. (1990). "A Theory of the Effects of Advanced Information Technologies on Organizational Design, Intelligence, and Decision Making". *Academy of Management Review,* **5**(1), pp.

47-91.

Håkanson, H. (1989).*Corporate technological Behavior-Corporation and Networks*, Pinter, London.

Itami, H. & Roehl, T.W. (1987). *Mobilizing invisible assets*. Harvard University Press, Cambridge,MA.

Jacobsen, R. (1992). "The Austrian school of strategy" *Academy of Management Review*, **17**(4), pp. 782-807.

Karakaya, F., and Kobu, F. (1994). "New product development processes- an investigation of success and failure in high-technology and non-high technology firms". *Journal of Business Venturing,* **9**(1), pp. 49-66.

Kefalas, A., and Schodebek, P.P. (1973). "Scanning the business environment, some empirical results". *Decision Science,* **4**, pp. 63-74.

Kim. J., and Mueller, C. W. (1978). *Factor analysis: Statistical methods and practical issues.* Beverly Hills, CA: Sage.

Kessler, E.H. and A.K. Chacrabarti, A.K. (1996). "Innovation speed: A conceptual model of context, antecedents, and outcomes", *Academy of Management Review*, **21**(4), pp. 1143-1191.

Kirzner, I.M. (1976). "On the method of Austrian economics". In E.G. Dolan (ed.). *The foundation of modern Austrian economics*, Sheed & Ward, Kansas City, MO, pp. 50-51.

Kirzner, I.M. (1985). *Discovery and the Capitalist Process.* University of Chicago Press, Chicago.

Kogut, B., and Zander, U. (1992). "Knowledge of the firm, combinative capabilities, and the replication of technology". *Organization Science*, **3**(3), pp. 383-397.

Kotabe, M., and Swan, K. S. (1995). "The role of strategic alliances in high technology new product development". Strategic Management Journal, **16**(8), pp. 621-636.

Kruger, L.J., and Struzziero, J. (1997). "Computer-mediated peer support of consultation: Case description and evaluation". *Journal of Educational and Psychological Consultation.* **8**(1), pp.75-90.

Krugman, P. (1995). Development, geography, and economic theory, The MIT Press, Boston.

Kurke, L.B., and Aldrich, H.E. (1983). "Mintzberg was right!: A replication and extension of the nature of managerial work". *Management Science*, **29**, pp. 975-984.

Lado, A. A., Boad, N.G., and Wright, P. (1992). "A competency-Based model of sustainable competitive advantage: Toward a conceptual integration". *Journal of Management*, **18**(1), pp. 77-91.

Lee, A.S. (1994). "Electronic mail as a medium for rich communication: an empirical investigation using hermeneutic interpretation". *MIS Quarterly,* **18**(2), June, pp. 143-157.

Leonard-Barton, D. (1995). *Wellsprings of knowledge: Building and sustaining the sources of innovation.* Harvard Business School Press, Boston, MA.

Liebeskind, J.P. (1996). "Knowledge, Strategy, and the theory of the firm". *Strategic Management* Journal, **17** (Winter Special Issue), pp. 93-107.

Link, A and Rees, J. (1991). "Firm size, university based research and the returns to R&D". *Small Business Economics*, **2**, pp. 25-32.

Lippman, S., and Rumelt, P. (1982). "Uncertain imitability: An analysis of interfirm differences in profitability under competition". *Bell Journal of Economics*, **13**, pp. 418-438.

Loveman, G.W. (1994). "An assessment of the productivity impact on information technologies". In T.J. Allen and M.S. Scott Morton (eds.). *Information technology and the corporation of the 1990's: Research studies*, MIT-Press, Cambridge, MA, pp. 84-111.

Lundvall, B.Å. (1988). "Innovation as an interactive process from User-producer interaction to the national system of innovation". In G. Dosi, C.Freeman, R.Nelson, G. Silverberg & L. Soete (eds.), *Technical Change and Economic Theory,* Pinter, London. pp. 349-370

Lumpkin, G.T., and Dess, G.G. (1996). "Clarifying the entrepreneurial orientation construct and linking it to performance". *Academy of Management Review,* **21**(1), pp. 135-172

MacPherson, A.D. (1992), "Innovation, External Linkages and Small Firm Commercial Performance", *Entrepreneurship & Regional Development*, **3**, pp. 165-181.

Markus, M.L. (1994). "Electronic mail as the medium of managerial choice". *Organization Science,* **5**(4), pp. 502-527.

Maturana, H.R. & Varela, F.J. (1987).The tree of Knowledge, New Science Library, London.

Moenaret, R.K., and Caeldries, F. (1996). "Architectural redesign, interpersonal communication, and learning in R&D". *Journal of Product Innovation Management,* **13**(4), pp. 296-310.

Morrison, C.J., Berndt, E.R. (1990). "Assessing the productivity of information technology equipment in the US. Manufacturing industries", *National Bureau of economic research*, Working Chapter 3582, January.

Mowery, D., and Rosenberg, N. (1979). "The Influence of Market Demand upon innovation: A critical review of some recent empirical studies", *Research Policy*, **8**(2), pp. 193-241.

Myers, S., and Marquis, D.G. (1969). *Successful industrial innovation.* National Science Foundation, Washington.

Nelson, R.R., and Winter, S.G. (1982). *An Evolutionary theory of economic change.* Belknap Press, Cambridge, MA.

Newell, S., and Swan, J. (1995). "Professional-associations as important mediators of the innovation process". *Science Communication,* **16**(4), pp. 371-387.

Nonaka, I. (1991). "The Knowledge creating company", *Harvard Business Review*, Nov.- dec.

Nonaka, I. (1994). "A dynamic theory of organizational knowledge creation". *Organizational Science*, **5**(1), pp. 14-37.

Nonaka, I., and Takeuchi, H. (1995). *The Knowledge Creating Company*, Oxford University Press, Oxford.

Nonaka, I., Umemot, K., and Senoo, D. (1996). "From information processing to knowledge creation: A paradigm shift in business management". *Technology in Society,* **18**(2), pp.203-218.

Nooteboom, B. (1994)."Innovation and Diffusion in Small Firms: Theory and Evidence". *Small Business Economics,* **6**, pp. 327-347.

Nunnally, J. C. (1978). *Psychometric theory (2nd ed.).* New York: McGraw-Hill.

OECD, (1988). *The Technologies in the 1990's: A Socio-Economic Strategy* (Sundquist Report), Paris, OECD.

Penrose, E.T. (1959). *The theory of the growth of the firm*. John Wiley and Sons, New York.

Pentland, B.T., and Rueter, H.H. (1994). "Organizational routines as grammars of action". *Administrative Science Quarterly*, **39**, pp. 484-510.

Pisano, G.P. (1994). "Knowledge integration, and the locus of learning: An empirical analysis of process development". *Strategic Management Journal*, **15** (Winter Special Issue), pp. 85-100.

Polanyi, M. (1966). *The tacit dimension*. Routledge & Kegan Paul, London.

Polanyi, M. (1983). The tacit dimension. Peter Smith, Gloucester, Mass.

Porter, M. (1980). *Competitive strategy*. Free Press, New York.

Porter, M.(1990). The competitive advantage of nations, Free Press, New York.

Porter, M.(1998). On competition, A Harvard Business Review Book, Boston.

Porter, M. (2002). Enhancing the microeconomic foundations of prosperity: The current competitiveness index. In Porter, M.E.; Sachs, J.D.; Cornelius, P.K.; McArthur, J.W. & Schwabb, K. The global competitiveness report 2001-2002, Oxford University Press, Oxford (pp. 52-76).

Powell, T.C., and Dent-Micallef, A. (1997). "Information technology as competitive advantage: The role of human, business and technology resources", *Strategic Management Journal,* **18**(5), pp. 375-405

Powell, W. (1990). "Neither market nor hierarchy: Network forms of organization". *Research in Organizational Behavior*, **12**, pp. 295-336.

Prahlad, C.K., and Hamel, G. (1990). "The Core Competence of the Corporation". *Harvard Business Review*, *68*, May-June, pp. 79-91.

Premkumar, G., and Ramamurthy, K. (1995). "The role of interorganizational and organizational factors on the decision mode for adaption of interorganizational systems". *Decision Science*, **26**(3) May-June, pp.303-336.

Quinn, J.B. (1992). *Intelligent Enterprise.* The Free Press, New York.

Quinn, J. B., Anderson, P., and Finkelstein, S. (1996). "Leveraging intellect". *Academy of Management Executive*, **10**(3), pp. 7-27.

Rauch, J. (1993). Productivity gains from geographic concentration of human capital: Evidence from the cities, Journal of Urban Economics,34, 3: 380-400.

Reed, R. and DeFillipi, R.J. (1990). "Causal ambiguity, barriers to imitation, and sustainable competitive advantage". *Academy of Management Review*, **15**(1), pp. 88-102.

Rolf, B. (1995). *Profession, tradition och tyst kunskap*, Nya Doxa, Nora, Sverige

Romer, P.M. (1986). "Increasing returns and long run growth" *Journal of Political Economy*, **94,** pp. 1002-1037.

Saxenian, A. (1994). *Regional Advantage*, Harvard University Press, Cambridge, MA.

Schendel, D. (1996). "Knowledge and the firm". *Strategic Management Journal*, **17**, special issue winter, pp.1-4.

Schumpeter, J.A. (1909). *Theorie der wirtschaftlichen Entwicklung.* Lepzig: Duncer & Humblot.

Schumpeter, J. (1934). *The theory of economic development.* Harvard University Press, Cambridge: Mass.

Schumpeter, J.A. (1939). *Business Cycles: A Theoretical, Historical and Statistical Analysis of the Capitalist Process,* 2 vols., McGraw Hill, New York.

Schumpeter, J.A. (1943). *Capitalism, Socialism and Democracy.* Unwin, London.

Slaughter, S. (1993). "Innovation and learning during implementation: a comparison of user and manufacturer innovation". *Research Policy,* **22**(1), pp. 81-97.

Solow, R.M. (1997). *Learning from learning by doing: Lessons for economic growth.* Stanford University Press, Stanford, California.

Song, X.M., Souder, W.E., and Dyer, B. (1997). "A causal model of the impact of skills, synergy and design sensitivity on new product performance". *Journal of Product Innovation Management,* **14** (2), pp. 88-101.

Spender, J-C. (1996). "Making knowledge the basis of a dynamic theory of the firm". *Strategic Management Journal,* **17** (Winter Special Issue), pp. 45-62.

Spender, J-C. and Grant, R.M. (1996). "Knowledge and the firm: Overview". *Strategic Management Journal*, **17** (Winter Special Issue), pp. 5-9.

Stewart, T.A. (1997). *Intellectual capital: The new wealth of organizations*. Doubleday, London.

Strassman, P.A. (1990). *Business value of computers*, Information Economic Press, New Canaar, C.T.

Sveiby, K.E. (1997). *The new organizational wealth: managing & measuring knowledge-based assets*, Berrett-Koehler, San Francisco.

Sweeney, G. (1996). "Learning efficiency, technological change and economic progress". *International Journal of Technology Management*, **11**(1-2), pp. 5-27.

Thurik, A.R (1996). "Introduction: Innovation and Small Business". *Small Business Economics,* **8**, pp. 175-176.

Thurow, L.C. (1996). *The future of capitalism*. Nicolas Brealey Publishing, London.

Tsoukas, H. (1996). "The firm as a distributed knowledge system: A constructionist approach". *Strategic Management Journal*, **17**

(Winter special Issue), pp.11-25.

Tushman, M.L. (1977). "Special Boundary Roles in the Innovation Process", *Administrative Science Quarterly*, **22**, December, pp.587-605.

Tushmann, M.L. og T.J.Scanlan (1981). "Boundary Spanning Individuals: Their Role in Information Transfer and their Antecedents". *Academy of Management Journal*, **24**(2), pp. 289-305.

Utterback, J. M. and W.J. Abernathy (1975). "A dynamic model of process and product innovation". *Omega*, **3**(6), pp. 639-656.

Van de Ven, A.H. (1986). "Central problems in the management of innovation", *Management Science*, **32**(5), pp. 590-607.

Volberda, H.W. (1996). "Towards the flexible form: How to remain vital in hypercompetitive environments". *Organizational Science*, 7(4), pp. 359- 374.

Von Hippel, E. (1987). "Corporation between rivals: informal know-how trading". *Research Policy*, **16**(5), pp 291-302.

Von Hippel, E. (1988). *The Sources of innovation.* Oxford University Press, Oxford.

Wade, J. (1996). "A community-level analysis of sources and rates of technological variation in the microprocessor market", *Academy of Management Journal*, **39**(5), pp. 1218-1244.

Wilson, D. (1993). "Assessing the impact of information technology on organizational performance", In R. Barker., R. Kauffman and M.A. Mahmoad (eds.). *Strategic information and technology management*, Idea Group, Harrisburg, PA.

Zaltman, G., R. Dunchan and J. Holbek (1973). *Innovations and organizations*, John Wiley, New York.

Zaremba, A. (1996). "Effects of e-mail availability on the informal network". *International Journal of Technology Management*. **11**(1-2), pp.151-161.

Zucker, L. (1991). "Markets for Bureaucratic Authority and control: Information quality in professions and services". *Research in the Sociology of Organization*, **8**, pp. 157-190.

Chapter on concepts

Ambidextrous organizations. *Ambidextrous organizations* are organizations that have the ability to adapt to changes in external conditions while at the same time generating their own future by means of, among other things, performance improvement, growth and innovation (Duncan, 1976; O'Reilly & Tushman, 2004, 2006, 2011; Thota & Munir, 2011). In chapter 6, we have shown how ambidextrous organizations can be developed by HR departments.

In 2004, O'Reilly & Tushman expressed that ambidextrous organizations would constitute one of the major challenges for management in the global knowledge economy.

The findings of O'Reilly & Tushman (2004) were overwhelming. Regarding the launching of radical innovations, they found that none of the cross-functional or unsupported teams and only a quarter of the teams with functional designs were able to produce radical innovations. However, among the ambidextrous organizations, 90% were successful in producing radical innovations. Empirical research has shown that this type of organizational design is best for producing both incremental and radical innovations (Thora & Munir, 2011).

Asplund's motivation theory[1]. In brief, this theory can be described in the following way: *People are motivated by social responses* (Asplund, 2010: 221-229). The following statement may be said to be a central point made by Asplund's theory: *When people receive social responses, their level of activity increases.*

Asplund's motivation theory is consistent with North's action theory (ref. North's action theory). Understood in this way, it seems reasonable to connect the two theories in the statement: *People are motivated by the social responses rewarded by the institutional framework.*

Availability cascades. This refers to the idea that we are all controlled by the image of reality created by the media, because this image is easy to retrieve from memory.

---

[1] Asplund's motivation theory, a term we use here, is based on Asplund's research..

Availability proposition. This may be expressed as follow: The more easily information enters into our consciousness, the greater the likelihood that we will have confidence in that information. In other words, we believe more in the type of information that is available in memory than the information that is not so readily available.

Behavioural perspective. This perspective focuses on the behaviour of employees as an explanation for the relationship between business strategy and the results obtained.

Boudon-Coleman diagram. This research methodology was developed by Mario Bunge (Bunge, 1978:76-79) based on insights made by the sociologists Boudon and Coleman. The purpose of the diagram is to show the relationship between the various levels, such as the macro and micro-levels. For instance, it is shown how changes at the macro-level, such as technological innovations in feudal society, can lead to increased income at the micro-level. However, it was shown that technological innovations could lead to weakening of the semi-feudal structures because dependency on land owners was reduced. Consequently, the landowners opposed such changes especially in the case of technological innovations, which Boudon has shown in his research (Boudon, 1981: 100). Coleman (Coleman, 1990: 7-12) started at the macro level, went to the individual level to find explanations and finally ended up at the macro level again.

An important purpose of Bunge's Boudon-Coleman diagram is to identify social mechanisms that maintain or change the phenomenon or problem under investigation (as mentioned above, in Boudon's analysis of semi-feudal society). Bunge's Boudon-Coleman diagram may be said to represent a "mixed strategy"; Bunge says the following: *When studying systems of any kind a) reduce them to their components (at some level) and the interaction among these, as well as among them and environmental items, but acknowledge and explain emergence* (see the chapter on concepts) *whenever it occurs, and b) approach systems from all pertinent sides and on all relevant levels, integrating theories or even research fields whenever unidisciplinarity proves to be insufficient* (Bunge, 1998:78). The purpose of this research strategy is to arrive at a deeper and more complete explanation of a system's behaviour.

Capabilities. Capabilities are for an organization what abilities are for an individual.

An organizational capability may thus be defined as an organization's ability to perform a task, activity or process. Operational capabilities enable an organization to make money in the here and now (Winter, 2003: 991-995). Dynamic capabilities, as opposed to operational capabilities, are linked to processes of change. Change and innovation are at the centre of dynamic capabilities.

Simplified, one may say that organizational capabilities are something an organization does well compared to its competitors (Ulrich and Brockbank, 2005). These capabilities are intangible and therefore difficult for competitors to imitate (Wernerfelt, 1984).

Cohesive energy. In a social system cohesive energy is "the glue" that binds the system together. Cohesive energy is the social mechanisms that make the system durable. According to systemic thinking it is the relationships and actions that bind social systems together. The rationale is that relationships and the systems of relationships may be said to control human behaviour. Social systems are held together (in systemic thinking) by dynamic social relations (e.g. feelings, perceptions, norms) and social action (e.g. cooperation, solidarity, conflict and communication).

Co-creation. Co-creation involves working together to promote knowledge processes and innovation. If knowledge processes and innovation are essential for value creation in the knowledge society, co-creation is an important social mechanism for initiating, maintaining and strengthening these processes. The balance between competition and cooperation, embodied in the concept of co-creation, leads to constructive criticism and the necessary scope of knowledge that exists in the network so as to promote creativity and the innovative. Instead of a zero-sum situation, a positive-sum situation will be developed where everyone wins.

Collective blindness. Collective blindness may be said to be a form of collective arrogance, which results in irrational actions. Minor events slip under the radar, causing the system to not be fully aware of what is happening. Politicians' explanations why voters in a referendum vote contrary to what most of the power elite and the media advocated is an example of collective blindness.

Competence. Competence refers to knowledge, skills and attitudes.

Core Competence. The concept was popular in the strategy literature of the 1990s. Core competence may be defined as: *"a bundle of skills and technologies that enable a company to provide a particular benefit to customers"* (Hamel & Prahalad, 1996:219). More recently, core competence as a concept has been given less attention in the research on dynamic capabilities, and now there is more focus on the concept of *fitness*. The term *evolutionary fitness* is also used in the research literature in connection with technology, quality, cost development, market development, innovation and competitive positioning (Helfat, et al, 2007: 7).

Discontinuous innovations. These are innovations that change the premises of technology, markets, our mindset, and so on. We know that sooner or later discontinuous innovations will emerge in the future (Hewing, 2013).

Dynamic capabilities. Dynamic capabilities stem from the resource-based perspective and evolutionary thinking in strategy literature (Teece,

2013: 3-65; 82-113; Nelson and Winter, 1982). The dynamic perspective attempts to explain what promotes an organization's competitive position over time through innovation and growth (Teece, 2013: x).

The original thinking concerning dynamic capabilities may be related to Teece et al. (1997). These authors defined dynamic capabilities as *an organization's ability to create, develop and modify its internal and external expertise in order to address changes in the external world.*

Dynamic capabilities are now seen as all the organizational processes, not only internal and external expertise, that contribute to an organization's capacity to adapt to change while creating the organization's future.

Explicit knowledge. This is knowledge that can be digitized and communicated to others as information.

Evidence. This may be results, such as research results, that can be relied on. However, it is also important to be aware of the fact that other evidence may be available without having to refer to figures and quantities, such as evidence that emerges from observations and good judgment without the assessment being quantified. Evidence-based research is research results that are based on approved and accepted scientific research methods.

Emergent. An emergent occurs if something new turns up on one level that has not previously existed on the level below. With emergent we mean: *Let S be a system with composition A, i.e. the various components in addition to the way they are composed. If P is a property of S, P is emergent with regard to A, if and only if no components in A possess P; otherwise P is to be regarded as a resulting property with regards to A.* (Bunge, 1977:97).

Entrepreneurial spirit. The entrepreneurial spirit may be described as follows (Roddick, 2003: 106-107):

- The vision of something new and belief in this that is so strong that belief becomes reality.
- A touch of positive madness.
- The ability to stand out from the crowd.
- Creative tension bubbling over.

- Pathological optimism.
- To act before you know!
- Basic desire for change.
- Creative energy focused on ideas, not on explicit factual knowledge.
- Being able to tell the story you want to sell.

Feedback Giving the other person feedback, for instance with regard to their behaviour, attitudes, and the like, is the most important element in the area of interactive skills and emotional intelligence (Goleman, 1996; 2007). Analysis of feedback is a sure way to identify our strengths and then reinforce them (Wang, et al., 2003). Failure to give people feedback on their behavior in some contexts may even be considered immoral.

Feed-forward. Feed-forward is regarded here as an expectation mechanism. It seems reasonable to assume that our expectations influence our behaviour in the present. It is therefore important that we make explicit to ourselves the expectations we have of a situation. By making expectations explicit, we have a greater opportunity to learn from our experiences and thus improve our performance.

Front line focus. This refers to those in the front line, i.e. in direct contact with customers, users, patients, students, etc. They have the greatest expertise, necessary information, and decision-making authority and are regarded as the most important resource in the organization because they are at the point where an organization's value creation occurs.

Global competence network. These competence networks may be divided into political, social, economic, technological and cultural patterns. It is when these five patterns interact that one may perceive the overall pattern. In the global knowledge economy it seems reasonable to assume that those who control this pattern set the conditions for economic development. These global competence networks will most likely make an impact on HR departments in companies competing for this kind of expertise in national markets.

Global competence networks are also emphasized as crucial for economic growth by OECD (2001), although they use the term *innovative clusters*. The purpose of innovative clusters and global competence networks is the development, dissemination and use of new ideas that promote wealth creation.

There is much to suggest that a greater degree of integration and cooperation between private and public sectors at the national and regional levels is an important prerequisite for initiating the innovative locomotive effect. The global competence networks are metaphorically the energy source that sustains the motion of this locomotive. It would be counterproductive to replace the locomotive once in motion. Conversely, the individual carriages of the locomotive (read: organizational level) can be changed depending on their competitive position. The individual passengers on the train create ideas and knowledge through the processes that may be called *creative chaos*. In this way we will arrive at a tripartite of the prerequisites for global competence networks. At the individual level, creative chaos occurs. At the organizational level, there will be creative destruction. At the social and global levels, creative collaboration takes place. These three processes create innovation and economic growth as an emergent, not as a *future perfectum*, i.e. a planned process with given results.

A prerequisite for the reasoning above is that tension and competition at one level requires collaboration at another level. Competition and cooperation are both necessary if one is to develop innovation and economic growth, in the same manner that stability and change are necessary for flexibility. Too much of the one (stability) leads to rigidity, and too much of the other (change) leads to chaos. Understood in this way, emergents cannot be planned.

Hamel's Law of Innovation. The "law" states that only between one and two of one thousand ideas become innovations in a market (Hamel, 2002; 2012). Therefore, an infostructure must be created to ensure that ideas are continuously produced in a business.

Hidden knowledge. Hidden knowledge is what we do not know we do not know. Kirzner (1982) says that hidden knowledge is possibly the most important knowledge domain of creativity, innovation and entrepreneurship.

History's "slow fields".

This refers to the fact that norms, values and actions tend to be in operation long after the functions, activities and processes that initially created them disappear, thus generating so-called *slow fields of history*. These norms, values and actions exist though they have no apparent function, contributing to maintaining a type of behaviour long after the type of behaviour is functional or meaningful[2]. For sociologists and historians it is important to determine whether norms and values have any function, or whether they are part of history's slow fields. By examining history's slow fields, it may be possible to provide better explanations for phenomena.

HR management. HR management is defined as HR practices at various levels (micro, meso, macro) for managing people in organizations.

HR management has been defined in many different ways. For instance, Boxall and Purcell (2003:1) define HR management as all those activities oriented towards managing relations between employees in an organization. This definition emphasizes the relational perspective. Later, they expanded their definition to include all the activities and processes that underpin an organization's value creation (Boxall and Purcell, 2010:29). On this basis, Armstrong defines the activities and processes

---

[2] Asplund (1970: 55) refers to a similar phenomenon when he discusses Simmel. He points out that the norms that may have had a positive function during a historic phase become in a later phase dysfunctional.

that HR management should engage in: *"HRM covers activities such as human capital management, knowledge management, organizational design and development, resource planning (recruitment, talent development), performance management, organizational learning, reward systems, relationships between employees, and employees' wellness."* (Armstrong, 2014:6). However, we believe Armstrong underestimates two essential areas of knowledge in his definition: the management of innovation processes, and change processes in organizations. Innovation and change are strongly emphasized in the global HRM Survey (White & Younger, 2013:35-39). Armstrong has included the ethical perspective in his Handbook for HRM (Armstrong, 2014a:95-105). Management of innovation processes and change processes in organizations is also highlighted and underlined by Wright et al. (2011: 5) in their description of HRM. However, it must also be said that Armstrong discusses innovation (Armstrong, 2014:145-155), but not in his process definition of HR management. Innovation and change processes are also emphasized by Ulrich et al. (2013). Brockbank (2013: 24) especially mentions these two processes as being important in the research model Ulrich et al. (2013) have developed through their empirical research over 25 years.

Implicit Knowledge. This is knowledge that is spread throughout an organization but not integrated.

Information input overload. This occurs when an individual, a team, an organization or a community receive more information than they can manage to process.

In a situation characterised by information input overload the following may occur (Miller, 1978: 123):

1. Designated tasks and responsibilities are left undone
2. Errors are made
3. Queues of information occur
4. Information is filtered out that should have been included
5. Abstract formulations are made when they should have been specific
6. Communication channels are overloaded, creating stress and tension in the system
7. Complex situations are shunned
8. Information is lumped together for processing

Each of the above eight points may result in a decrease in efficiency when the system is exposed to information input overload.

Infostructure. The infostructure concerns the processes that enable the development, transfer, analysis, storage, coordination and management of data, information and knowledge. The infostructure consists of eleven generic processes, as shown in Fig. 8 in this book. The eleven processes in the infostructure may be considered as nodes in a social network at different levels, for example team, organization, society, and region, all in the global space. Together, the eleven processes comprise the totality of the infostructure.

It may be said that the *info*structure has the same importance in the knowledge society as the *infra*structure had in the industrial society.

Innovation. Innovation is here understood as any idea, practice or material element, which is perceived as new for the person using it (Zaltman et al., 1973).

Ideas are seen as the smallest unit in the innovation process (Hamel, 2002; 2012). However, this refers to the ideas that are in process of development and not fully developed ideas. Before an idea can be characterized as innovative, it must prove to be beneficial to somebody, i.e. the market must accept the idea and apply it. Consequently, the creative process of innovation is here understood as the benefit it has for a market (Amabile, 1990; Johannessen, et al., 2001: 25). Thus, it is not sufficient that an idea is new for it to be considered an innovation. An idea may have a great degree of novelty, but if it is of no benefit to anybody in the market, then it has no innovative value.

Kaizen. This is a Japanese method, which means that an organization develops systems for organized improvement (Maurer, 2012).

Knowledge. The definition of knowledge used here is *the systematization and structuring of information for one or more goals or purposes.*

Knowledge worker. A knowledge worker has been described by the OECD as *a person whose primary task is to generate and apply knowledge*, rather than to provide services or produce physical products (OECD, 2000 a, b, c, d, e; 2001). This may be understood as a *formal definition* of a knowledge worker.

This definition does not restrict knowledge workers to creative fields, as is the case with, for example, Mosco and McKercher (2007: vii–xxiv). The OECD definition also allows for the fact that a knowledge worker may perform routine tasks. The definition also does not limit the type of work performed by knowledge workers to tasks relating to creative problem-solving strategies, unlike the definition provided by Reinhardt et al. (2011).

Knowledge enterprise. This is an enterprise that has knowledge as its most significant output. It is perhaps helpful to think of the process *input - process - output* to separate industrial enterprises from knowledge enterprises. Much knowledge and skills are needed to produce high-tech products such as computers, and there are also many knowledge workers involved in this process. However, the majority of products produced today are high-tech industrial products, and although such products require very skilled knowledge in the production process, they are nevertheless output-industrial products.

On the other hand, law firms, consulting firms and universities are examples of knowledge enterprises.

Knowledge management. Management of knowledge resources in an organization. These resources may be explicit knowledge, implicit knowledge, tacit knowledge and hidden knowledge.

Locomotive effect. This refers to something that generates and then reinforces an activity or development.

Modularization. An extreme fragmentation of the production process in the global knowledge economy. Production is fragmented and distributed according to the following logic: Costs – quality – competence – design – innovation.

Modular flexibility. The modulization of value creation. Modular flexibility may best be understood as the globalization of production processes, and extreme specialization of work processes with a focus on core processes.

Necessary and sufficient conditions. It may often be appropriate to divide conditions or premises into *necessary conditions* and *sufficient* *conditions*. Necessary conditions must be present to trigger an action, but these may not be sufficient. The sufficient conditions must also be present to trigger the action.

North's action theory[3]. This action theory may be expressed in the following statement: *People act on the basis of a system of rewards as expressed in the norms, values, rules and attitudes in the culture (the institutional framework)* (North, 1990; 1993). North's action theory is also consistent with Asplund's motivation theory (ref. Asplund's motivation theory).

Primary task. An organization's primary task is what the system is designed to do.

Proposition. This is an overarching hypothesis. It says something about the relationship between several variables. A proposition relates to a hypothesis in the same way the main research problem relates to research questions.

---

[3] North's action theory is a term we use here based on North's research.

Punctuation. By punctuation (Bateson, 1972:292-293) a distinction is drawn between cause and effect; this is done with a clear motive in mind. A causality is thus created which does not actually exist in the real world, and one is then free to discuss the effects of this cause which has been created through a process of punctuation.

A sequence of a process is selected, and then bracketed. In this way, we de-limit what is punctuated from the rest of the process. Figuratively, we may imagine this as a circle that is divided into small pieces; one piece of the circle is then selected and folded out into a straight line. This results in the creation of an artificial beginning and end. This beginning and end of course cannot exist in a circle, but only through the process of punctuation.

Social laws. Social laws constitute a pattern of a unique type. They are systemic and connected to a system of knowledge, and cannot change without the facts they represent also being changed (Bunge, 1983; 1983a). The main differences between a statement of a law and other statements are:

1. Law statements are general.

2. Law statements are systemic, i.e. they are related to the established

system of knowledge.

3. Law statements have been verified through many studies.

A pattern may be understood as variables that are stable over a specific period of time. A social law is created when an observer gains insight into the pattern. By gaining such insight, we can also predict parts of behaviour or at least develop a rough estimate within a short period of time.

Social laws are further related to specific social systems, both in time and space. However, this does not represent any objection to social laws, because this is also true of natural laws (although these have a longer time span and are of a more general nature).

Social mechanism. Robert Merton (1967) brought the notion of social mechanisms into sociology, although we can find rudiments of this in both Weber – with the Protestant ethic as an explanation for the emergence of capitalism in Europe – and in Durkheim, who uses society as an explanation for a rising suicide rate. For Merton, social mechanisms are the building blocks of *middle range theories*. He defines social mechanisms as *social processes having designated consequences* *for designated parts of the social structure* (Merton, 1968:43). In the 1980s and 1990s, Jon Elster developed a new notion of the role of social mechanisms in sociology (Elster, 1983;1989). Hedstrom and Swedberg write that, *the advancement of social theory calls for an analytical approach that systematically seeks to explicate the social mechanisms that generate and explain observed associations between events* (Hedstrøm & Swedberg, 1998:1).

It is one thing to point out connections between phenomena. It is something quite different to point out satisfactory explanations for these relationships, which is what social mechanisms accomplish. A social mechanism tells us what will happen, how it will happen and why it will happen (Bunge, 1967). Social mechanisms are primarily analytical constructs which cannot necessarily be observed; in other words, they are epistemological, not ontological. However, social mechanisms are observable in their consequences. An intention can be a social mechanism of action. We cannot observe an intention, but we can interpret it in light of the consequences manifested through an action. Preferences can also function as a social mechanism for economic behaviour. We cannot observe a person's preferences, but we can interpret them in the light of the behavioural consequences that manifest themselves. Social mechanisms are, understood in this way, analytical constructs, indicating connections between events (Hernes, 1998).

Bunge says: *"... a social mechanism is a process in a concrete system, such that it is capable of being about or preventing some change in the system as a whole or in some of its subsystems"* (Bunge, 1997:414). By 'social mechanism' here we mean those activities that promote/inhibit social processes in relation to a specific problem / phenomenon.

Material resources and technology are social mechanisms of the economic subsystem; power is a social mechanism of the political subsystem; fundamental norms and values are a social mechanism of the cultural subsystem; and human relationships are a social mechanism of the social subsystem. These system-specific social mechanisms interact with each other to achieve certain goals, maintain these systems, or to avoid certain undesirable conditions in the system or the outside world.

The difficulty of discovering social mechanisms and distinguishing them from processes may be partly explained by the fact that social mechanisms are also processes (Bunge, 1997:414). For the application of social mechanisms, see the Boudon-Coleman diagram.

Social system. From a systemic perspective, social systems can be conceptual or concrete. Theories and analytical models are examples of conceptual systems. Further, social systems are *composed of people and their artifacts* (Bunge, 1996:21). Social systems are held together (in systemic reasoning) by **dynamic social relations** (such as emotions, interpretations, norms, etc.) and **social actions** (such as, cooperation, solidarity, conflict and communication, etc.). None of the social actions have precedence in the systemic interpretation of social systems, such as conflict in the case of Marx, and solidarity in the case of Durkheim.

Staccato-behaviour (erratic behaviour). If organizations introduce too many change processes in succession too quickly, a phenomenon may occur called "staccato-behaviour".

If an organization does not deal with this appropriately, it seems reasonable to assume that workers will become tired, burnt-out and de-motivated. Perhaps most damaging to business, employees will lose focus on their primary task - what the business is designed to do. In addition, businesses will often experience that this leads to an increasing degree of opportunistic behaviour (Ulrich, 2013a:260).

Strategic HR management. Strategic HR management is defined in this book as: *The choices an HR department makes with regard to human resources for the purposes of achieving the organization's goals.* This is analogous to the view of Storey et al. (2009:3) and consistent with the definition we employ of HR management. This means that strategic HR management must be focused on the *micro, meso* and *macro-levels.*

There are many definitions of strategic HR management. For instance, *use of human resources in order to achieve lasting competitive advantages for the business* (Mathis and Jackson, 2008:36); *management of the employees, expressed through management philosophy, policy and praxis* (Torrington et al., 2005:28); *development of a consistent practices in order to support the strategic goals of the business* (Mello, 2006:152); *a complex system with the following characteristics: vertical integration, horizontal integration, efficiency, partnership* (Schuler and Jackson, 2005).

Systemic thinking. Systemic thinking makes a distinction between the epistemological sphere (Bunge, 1985), the ontological sphere (Bunge, 1983), the axiological sphere (Bunge, 1989, 1996) and the ethical sphere

(Bunge, 1989). Systemic thinking makes a clear distinction between intention and behaviour. Intention is something that should be *understood*, while behaviour is something that should be *explained*. To understand an intention we must study the historical factors, situations and contexts, as well as the expectation mechanisms. Behaviour must be explained with respect to the context, relationships and situation it unfolds in. What implication does the distinction between intention and behavior have for the study of social systems?

Interpretation of meaning is an important part of the *intention aspect* in the distinction. Explanation and prediction become an essential part of the *behavioral aspect* of the distinction.

In systemic thinking it is the link between the interpretation of meaning and explanation, and prediction, which provides historical and social sciences with practical strength. By making a distinction between intention and behaviour, the historical and the social sciences are interpretive, explanatory and predictive projects. According to systemic thinking, many of the contradictions in the historical and social sciences spring from the fact that a distinction is not made between intention and behaviour. The problem of the historical and social sciences is that the actors who are studied have both intentions and they also exercise types of behaviour; however, this isn't problematic as long as we make a distinction between intention and behaviour. By simultaneously introducing the distinction between intention and behaviour, systemic thinking has made it possible to identify, for instance, partial explanations from each of two main epistemological positions, namely, the naturalists and anti-naturalists (Johannessen & Olaisen, 2005; 2006), and synthesize these explanations into new knowledge.

Systemic thinking emphasizes circular causal processes, also called *interactive causal processes*, in addition to linear causal processes (Johannessen, 1996; 1997). Systemic thinking argues that to understand objective social facts, one must examine the subjective aspects of these. In systemic thinking, objective social facts exist, but they are often more difficult to grasp than facts in the natural world, because social facts are often influenced by expectations, emotions, prejudices, ideology and economic and social interests. *"Aspect-seeing"* is thus a way of approaching these social facts.

Emergents are central to systemic thinking. A pattern behind the problem or phenomenon is always sought in systemic investigations. Patterns may be revealed by studying the underlying processes that constitute a phenomenon or problem, *and the search for pattern is what scientific research is all about* (Bunge, 1996:42).

According to systemic thinking it is a misconception to say that the facts are social constructions. The misunderstanding involves confusing our *concepts* concerning facts and our *hypotheses* about the facts together with the facts. Our concepts and hypotheses are mental constructs. The facts, however, are not mental constructs. Social need, for instance, is not a social fact; it is a mental construct of, for instance, starvation. Starvation is a social fact. Social need is a mental or social construction. Not being able to read is a social fact. Illiteracy is, however, a social construction.

A *symbol* should symbolize something, just as a *concept* should delineate something. A *hypothesis* should explain something or express something about relationships. A conceptual *model* should say something about the relationships between concepts. A *theory* should say something about relationships between propositions. Physical or social facts are untouched by all these mental constructions. That one can through constructs change social facts, or that social facts are changed as a social consequence of using constructs, is neither original nor new.

The aim of theoretical research, according to the systemic position, is the construction of systems, i.e. theories (Bunge, 1974: v). The order in systemic research is thus: Theory - Analysis - Synthesis.

In the methodological sphere, the systemic position has its main focus on relationships, both in terms of concrete things, ideas and knowledge. Consequently, systemic thinking encourages interdisciplinary and multidisciplinary approaches to problems or phenomena.

The systemic position thus attempts to bridge the gap between methodological individualism and methodological collectivism, which is considered the classic controversy in historical- and social sciences.

The perceptions that an observer has about social systems will influence his/her actions, regardless of whether the perceptions are true or fallacious. Systemic investigations start, therefore, writes Bunge *from individuals embedded in a society that preexists them and watch how their actions affect society and alter it* (Bunge, 1996:241). The study of social systems from a systemic perspective for these reasons always includes the triad: actors - observers - social systems.

The observer tries to uncover a system's composition, environment and structure. Then the actors' subjective perception of composition, environment and structure are examined. In other words, both the subjective and objective aspects are studied. When we wish to study changes in social systems, from a systemic point of view, we have to examine the social mechanisms (drivers) that influence changes; both internal and external social mechanisms must be identified. This study takes place within the four subsystems: the economic, political, cultural and relational. According to systemic thinking, social changes occur along seven axes:

1. As an *expectation* of new relationships, values, power constellations, technologies and distribution of material resources.
2. As a result of our *beliefs* (mental models) about relationships, values, power constellations, technical and material resources.
3. As a result of *psychological elements*, such as: irritation, crisis, discomfort, unsatisfactory life, unworthy life, loss of well-being, etc.
4. As a result of *communication* in and between systems.
5. As a result of an *understanding of connections* (contextual understanding).
6. As a result of learning and new *self-knowledge*.
7. As a result of *new ideas* and ways of thinking.

Historiography, from a systemic perspective, has one clear goal: to investigate what happened, where it happened, when it happened, how it happened, why it happened, and with what results.

Systemic assumptions related to historiography and social sciences may be expressed in the following (Bunge 1998:263):

a. The past has existed.

b. Parts of the past can be known.

c. Every uncovering of the past will be incomplete.

d. New data, techniques, and systemizations and structuring will reveal new aspects of the past.

e. Historical knowledge is developed through new data, discoveries, hypotheses and approaches.

In systemic thinking if changes are to take place, then the material will sometimes be given precedence; at other times, ideology, ideas and thinking are given precedence. In other contexts, there is a systemic link between the material and ideas that is needed to bring about changes. In such contexts, it is difficult and irrelevant to say what is the primary driver, i.e. the material or ideas; this would be on par with discussing what came first, the chicken or the egg.

The processes that drive social change, according to a systemic perspective, are the interaction between the economic, political, relational and cultural subsystems. In some situations, one of these four perspectives will prevail, whereas in others it will be one or more of the four subsystems that are the drivers of social change. In many cases, it is precisely the interaction between the four subsystems that leads to social changes.

In this context the systemic perspective may be described by saying that material conditions/energy, such as economic relationships, may provide the ground from which ideologies develop, but that these ideologies in return influence the development of the material. Whether material conditions / energy or ideology comes first is often determined by a historiographical punctuation process (Bateson, 1972:163).

The systemic perspective balances historical materialism and historical idealism. It assumes that overall social changes are the result of economic, political, social and cultural factors, in addition to the interaction between material conditions / energy and ideas. Furthermore, a systemic perspective views any society as being interwoven into its surroundings (Bunge, 1998: 275). When a historian considers a historical situation – such as the massacre in Van in April 1915 – from this perspective then he is trying *to throw light upon the internal working of a past culture and society* (Stone, 1979: 19).

The systemic position attempts to view the relevant event in a larger context, in order to find *the patterns which combine* (Bateson, 1972:273-274), because *change depends upon feedback loop* (Bateson, 1972:274). Bunge says about this position: *By placing the particular in a sequence, adopting a broad perspective the systemist overcomes the idiographic/nomothetic duality, ..., as well as the concomitant narrative/structural opposition* (Bunge 1998:275). This means, metaphorically, that the systemic researcher uses a microscope, telescope and a helicopter to investigate patterns over time.

Systemic research strategy is a *zig-zagging between the micro-meso and macro levels* (Bunge, 1998:277). Through a systemic research strategy the researcher has ample opportunities to use a Boudon-Coleman diagram.

Systemic thinking examines four types of changes[4].

<u>Type I change</u> concerns individuals who change history, such as Genghis

---

[4] The four types of changes are related to Bateson's (1972:279-309) work on different types of learning, especially those discussed in his article *Logical types of learning and communication*.

Khan, Hitler, Stalin, Mao Zedong, etc.

Type II change concerns groups of people acting together who change history. Examples of Type II change include the invasion of the Roman Empire by peoples from the north; and the Ottoman expansion into the Balkans between the late 1400s and when the Ottoman Empire was pushed back partly due to nationalist liberation movements in the early 1900s.

Type III change include changes in history that are caused by natural disasters, such as the volcanic eruption that destroyed Pompeii. Climate change may also be said to an example of a type III change.

Type IV change involves a total change in the way of thinking, such as the emergence of new religions, like Islam, or a new political ideology, such as Marxism.

The systemic researcher attempts to explore the relationship between the four types of changes. A single event is in itself not necessarily of special interest to the systemic researcher; rather, the focus is on the *system of events* of which the single event is a part.

All the social sciences are used in the systemic position to seek insight, understanding and to explain a phenomenon or problem.

Tacit knowledge. Knowledge that is difficult to communicate to others as information. It is also very difficult, if at all possible, to digitize.

The knowledge-based perspective. The knowledge-based perspective is defined here as creating, expanding and modifying internal and external competencies to promote what the organization is designed to do (Grant, 2003: 203).

The resource-based perspective. This perspective can be defined as the structuring and systematization of the organization's internal *resources* so it is difficult for competitors to copy them.

Theory. Here understood as a system of propositions (Bunge, 1974: v).

INDEX

A

Armstrong, 151
attention, 7, 30, 32, 40, 42, 43, 61, 79, 105, 112, 143
Authorities, 94
authority, 11, 12, 147

B

Boudon-Coleman diagram, 139
Boudon-Colemandiagram, 171
Bunge, 145, 161, 168, 171

C

change, 8, 17, 18, 19, 26, 41, 47, 48, 55, 57, 63, 71, 72, 75, 93, 98, 99, 103, 123, 129, 134, 140, 141, 143, 144, 146, 149, 151, 158, 161, 162, 166, 170, 171, 172
channel capacity, 6, 8, 9, 10, 11, 13, 14, 15, 16, 17, 19, 22, 24, 25, 26
clusters, 91, 92, 93, 94, 148
communication, 7, 9, 11, 12, 14, 15, 16, 17, 19, 20, 21, 25, 27, 28, 29, 39, 44, 47, 49, 52, 53, 54, 55, 56, 64, 86, 87, 95, 96, 97, 100, 102, 104, 109, 119, 126, 128, 141, 162, 168, 172
communicative openness, 26
Competence, 50, 51, 72, 131, 143
competition, 16, 28, 29, 39, 59, 79, 80, 89, 90, 93, 111, 114, 127, 130, 142, 149
complementary, 7, 8, 16, 17, 22, 49, 89, 92, 94
connectance, 8, 18, 19, 20, 21, 22, 24, 25, 26, 33, 47, 64

D

democratic, 11, 12
density, 25, 92
diffusion, 50, 62, 71, 74, 75
disintegration, 94

E

Emergent, 145
endringer, 137, 144, 168, 170, 172, 173
endringsprosesser, 151, 162, 170
epistemology, 113
explicit, 7, 12, 32, 38, 49, 84, 85, 97, 101, 109, 113, 146, 147, 156
external factors, 44, 57

F

Face-to face, 29
feedback, 7, 25, 99, 100, 109, 146, 171
Feed-forward, 146
function, 7, 49, 112, 150, 161

H

holography, 53

I

idiosyncratic, 112
information, 6, 8, 9, 10, 11, 12, 13, 14, 15, 16, 17, 19, 20, 21, 25, 28, 30, 39, 44, 46, 47, 48, 49, 50, 52, 55, 57, 58, 64, 80, 81, 82, 83, 86, 87, 92, 95, 96, 97, 98, 99, 100, 101, 104, 105, 106, 107, 108, 110, 113, 116, 117, 118, 119, 120, 122, 123, 127, 128, 129, 136, 139, 144, 147, 152, 153, 154, 173
innovasjon, 137, 142, 144, 148, 149, 154, 156
innovation, iv, 5, 6, 7, 8, 13, 16, 17, 19, 20, 22, 24, 27, 29, 31, 37, 38, 39, 40, 41, 42, 43, 44, 45, 46, 48, 49, 50, 52, 53, 54, 55, 56, 57, 58, 59, 60, 61, 62, 63, 65, 66, 67, 68, 69, 70, 71, 73, 74, 75, 76, 79, 80, 82, 83, 85, 88, 93, 94, 95, 96, 100, 101, 104,105, 106, 108, 110, 113, 115, 119, 120, 121, 122, 123, 124, 126, 127, 128, 129, 133, 135, 136, 137, 141, 142, 143, 144, 148, 149, 151, 153, 156
innovative environment, 16
institutions, 42, 43, 60, 62, 90, 91, 94, 95
internal factors, 44, 45

K

knowledge, 6, 14, 23, 29, 30, 38, 39, 42, 43, 46, 48, 51, 54, 60, 61, 63, 79, 80, 81, 82, 83, 84, 85, 86, 87, 88, 95, 96, 98, 101, 104, 107, 108, 112, 115, 116, 121, 123, 124, 126, 129, 134, 135, 137, 142, 143, 144, 146, 147, 148, 149, 151, 152, 153, 154, 155, 156,158, 159, 165, 167, 169, 173 knowledge creation, 113

L

learning, 38, 39, 40, 43, 44, 45, 48, 53, 54, 56, 58, 60, 63, 69, 86, 87, 95, 96, 97, 102, 104, 106, 119, 128, 130, 133, 151, 169, 172

M

management, 8, 11, 12, 39, 44, 52, 53, 54, 56, 65, 67, 70, 75, 109, 117, 123, 129, 135, 136, 137, 150, 153, 156, 163, 177
media, 98, 100, 101, 102, 103, 108, 120, 138, 142

N

network, 31, 39, 43, 51, 56, 60, 62, 71, 98, 101, 109, 136, 142, 153

O

OECD, 148, 155
organisation, 6, 7, 8, 10, 11, 12, 13, 14, 15, 16, 17, 20, 22, 25, 28, 29, 31, 42, 45, 49, 50, 52, 54, 55

P

percolation, 83, 98, 104, 116
productivity, 43, 56, 91, 93, 94, 95, 118, 127, 128

R

resource-based view, 97, 111, 112
resources, 25, 29, 31, 38, 51, 81, 114, 131, 156, 161, 163, 168, 173

S

social, 21, 38, 48, 63, 83, 88, 89, 97, 102, 103, 110, 118, 138, 140, 141, 142, 147, 148, 153, 159, 160, 161, 162, 164, 165, 166, 167, 168, 169, 170, 173
structure, 11, 12, 13, 20, 41, 42, 55, 56, 67, 71, 74, 93, 95, 112, 160, 168
sufficient condition, 16
sustainability, 81, 101
system, 8, 17, 18, 19, 20, 22, 23, 24, 25, 26, 27, 31, 38, 39, 42, 45, 47, 48, 50, 52, 53, 54, 59, 61, 62, 63, 69, 87, 89, 90, 92, 97, 127, 135, 140, 141, 142, 145, 152, 153, 157, 158, 159, 161, 162, 163, 167, 173

T

tacit, 38, 46, 51, 84, 85, 86, 97, 101, 109, 113, 123, 130, 156
technology, 15, 39, 43, 44, 50, 54, 55, 57, 58, 60, 62, 70, 71, 72, 74, 75, 79, 93, 100, 103, 115, 118, 122, 124, 125, 127, 128, 131, 136, 143, 161
trigger, 97, 103, 110, 157

U

V

Ø

ABOUT THE AUTHOR

Jon-Arild Johannessen holds a Master of Science from Oslo University in History. He holds a Ph.D. from Stockholm University in Systemic thinking. He is currently professor (full) in Leadership, at Kristiania University College, Oslo and Nord University, Norway. He has been professor (full) in Innovation, at Syd-danske University, Denmark. He has been professor (full) in Management at The Arctic University, Norway. At Bodø Graduate School of Business, Norway he had a professorship (full) in Information management At Norwegian School of Management he has been professor in Knowledge Management.

www.ingramcontent.com/pod-product-compliance
Lightning Source LLC
Chambersburg PA
CBHW070240190526
45169CB00001B/236